The True Story of a Pilot and His Dog

SKIPPER

GOES TO

WAR

EUGENE & SERENE HACKEL

Brynmoor Books
an imprint of eFitzgerald Publishing, LLC

Table of Contents

To J. O. Leonard, Jr.
and his family for
providing the focus and
star of this story,
"SKIPPER"

Preface

When I first met my husband-to-be in 1947, he delighted me with stories about Skipper, his bomber crew mascot during World War II. Many times Skipper's escapades were retold at social gatherings. However, when I moved to Goshen, Connecticut and joined a writer's group, I decided to chronicle the adventures of this cocker spaniel.

As a new writer, working with someone else—especially when that someone is a husband—presented a challenge. Since it was his story, I felt it would work better to have him relate the anecdotes, after which I would copy down his words. However, in the telling, there seemed to be so much omitted. Asking questions brought out feelings that I had never heard about before, and many times as I tried to incorporate the crew's brash, positive outlook with what was really going on, tears welled up in my eyes. Finding a voice that rang true to the reactions of the young fliers, who fought during the frustrating period prior to the invasion of Normandy, was a hurdle that we had to cross. The result was a very special bonding that added a layer of understanding to a period we never shared as a couple. One thing led to another, and as I gained in confidence, we wrote additional chapters that further illuminated the true story of Eugene's wartime experience.

My husband and I printed hard cover copies of the book prior to Christmas 2004. Surprisingly, they all sold out, and families of the crew scrambled to buy extra copies to give to their relatives. Although we often talked of reprinting "Skipper," my husband became ill during the ensuing years, ending in his death in 2014. In honor of his service in World War II plus continuing requests for copies, I decided as his widow to keep this story of the crew's bravery in the face of fear alive for new generations.

—*Serene Hackel*
June 26, 2018
West Hartford, Connecticut

Acknowledgments

The idea of putting together the many vignettes about Skipper into book form actually came from a friend, Judy Hippner, whose delight in the little dog's adventures was filled with such enthusiasm that we were called on to repeat each tale over and over at separate social gatherings. We are grateful for her imagination and persistence.

We want to thank the Goshen Writers Group for their avid support, along with their constructive feedback. Northwest Writers also provided an audience and motivation for us to continue.

Important guidance toward keeping the action moving was contributed by Jean Sands. Susan Bria added to the mix by doing a masterful job of proofreading. Drs. Zuli and Susan Steremberg, who read the first draft, urged us to pursue publication with so much exuberance that it buoyed our confidence. We followed the suggestion of Jack Rabin, who felt that adding a chapter about Gene's inability to drive a car would enhance the story. Dr. Gene Gitelle's interest was also helpful.

"Bye Bye Blackbird" is used by permission of Old Cloverleaf Music Co. c/o Fred Ahlert and Henderson Music Co., Inc. c/o M. Wm. Krasilovsky, Copyright 1926.

A salute to Bob Porzio for recording many of the old snapshots on a compact disk.

Finally, we owe a debt of gratitude to Deborah Benner of Goose River Press, whose skill in the original formatting and production of this book was indispensible. The 2018 update of the book was handled by Patrice Fitzgerald of eFitzgerald Publishing, LLC.

—*Eugene and Serene Hackel*

SKIPPER

GOES TO

WAR

Eugene Hackel

CHAPTER ONE
Departing the U.S.A.

The swirling snow, illuminated by New York's 34th Street neon lights, made the world feel surreal to the young lieutenant. Gene could hardly believe that he would be leaving for the European Theatre of Operations within twenty-four hours. As he walked along briskly with Al Lages, his crew bombardier, the idea of flying to a war zone seemed like some crazy dream.

Suddenly, Al stopped. "Uh-oh. He has to pee," said Al, pointing to the little cocker spaniel he held at the end of a short leash.

"For God's sake," said Gene, "when's he going to learn to lift his leg instead of squatting like a girl?" He turned to the dog. "What kind of a crew mascot are you?"

The puppy looked up at him with limpid eyes, shivering from the collected snow on his golden eyebrows and soft black coat.

In a swift act of contrition, Gene swooped up the little dog and planted a kiss on his golden jowl. "I'm sorry, Skipper. You must be cold and scared."

He looked at his buddy. "Hey, Al! We're near Macy's. Let's go to the pet department and buy him a sweater. He'll probably need it where we're heading."

"We're some pair. Off to bomb Germany and we're worried about this little punk," said Al.

Macy's, crowded with Thursday night shoppers, brought a myriad of memories to Gene's mind. The aisles filled with merchandise, scents of perfume, and salesgirls' smiles had been a part of his childhood. How often had he held his mother's hand while browsing for clothes, gifts, toys, or a visit to Santa. The cheerful atmosphere made the war seem so remote. Yet he knew he would be joining his combat group in a few days.

The girl at the information desk directed them to the pet supply department. "It's on the eighth floor. Cute dog. Cute owner too," she muttered, lowering her eyes.

Gene felt proud of his uniform with its silver wings, and he enjoyed the attention it brought. Flying had been his dream since he was a kid in Washington Heights.

He thought back to the day when Japan had attacked Pearl Harbor. He was a machinist at the Norfolk Navy Yard in Virginia. Nineteen years old and overwhelmed with rage and fear for his country, he made up his mind then and there to become a bomber pilot in the United States Army Air Corps.

Relatives and friends raised their eyebrows when they learned he was giving up a draft-deferred job. Some questioned his judgment. But after his mother died three years ago, he had to make many decisions without consulting family. Now there was no turning back.

Skipper balked as they approached the escalator, pulling at the leash.

"I thought you were a brave little fella," Gene said.

Skipper trembled.

"Brave?" Al laughed. "That's a joke. I'm beginning to think it was a bad idea to try to take him with us."

A gift from the first pilot's sister, Skipper the pup had been with the plane's crew in Florida since he was eight weeks old. Now, three months later, he had wormed his way into each crew member's heart. At least, it seemed that way to Gene. "May I help you?" asked a redheaded salesgirl with curly bangs and a pageboy bob.

Gene put Skipper on the counter. "We need a sweater for him."

"Oh, my! How darling." The girl bent down to bury her face in the puppy's soft fur, her long hair covering his golden eyebrows. "What a dear!" she said, hugging the wiggling bundle. "What's his name?"

"Skipper," answered Al.

After a moment, the girl looked up into Gene's brown eyes and said, "We have so many styles; do you have anything particular in mind?"

"Let's see what you got."

A blond salesgirl from a nearby counter left her post and

hurried to take Skipper in her arms, making room to display several sweaters.

Gene placed a green and white plaid wool coat on Skipper's back. "Nope," he said. "He's a cocker spaniel, not a Scottish terrier."

Neither the imitation overcoats nor the sweaters trimmed with white piping seemed fitting for his small buddy, and Gene was about to give up when the blond held up a bright red sweater with a blue and white striped turtle neck collar.

"Here's just the right one!" she said, tugging it over Skipper's head. Several shoppers gathered to watch him try on his new sweater, smiling their approval.

"Doesn't he look adorable?" said the pleased redhead. Moments later, the pup rolled onto his back and pointed all four paws to the ceiling, with "Scratch my belly" written across his face.

"Look at the little flirt." Al laughed. "Now all we need is for one of you gals to sew an Air Force patch on each shoulder." He pulled a couple of them from his musette bag.

The blond salesgirl rummaged under the counter and found a tin box filled with various colored spools of thread. She chose a bright blue strand, deftly guided it through the needle's eye, and stitched the two patches in place. Skipper licked her nose and chin.

"How do you like this ladies' man?" said Al.

"Thank you, Miss," Gene said. "Skipper looks real fine, doesn't he, Al?"

"You look swell, Skipper." Al tucked the pup under his arm. They passed the information desk on the way out, and

Gene nodded to the young woman who had directed them to the pet department. "Bye now," he said with a smile.

"Yeah! Thanks a lot!" Al held Skipper in the air so she could see his new attire.

Outside, the snow had stopped.

"See you at Penn Station tomorrow morning on the 5:33 to Delaware," Gene said. "Let's meet at the gate."

Al hailed a cab that would take him and Skipper to Washington Heights in uptown Manhattan. He was the only married member of the crew, and Gene felt sad for him, knowing it would be a somber goodbye the next morning. Actually, he and Al were lucky to be able to spend this night with their families, who lived only a short train ride away from New Castle Field in Delaware, where they would be returning the next day. The other crewmembers were not so fortunate.

Gene stopped at the Chalfonte Hotel on 70th Street and Broadway. The cranberry canvas canopy, dusted with snow, gave the appearance of understated elegance, and the lobby glowed softly with lit sconces. Crackling logs burned in the fireplace.

A uniformed doorman with golden epaulets greeted him. "Good evening, Lieutenant. The desk clerk will make a call to announce your arrival."

Gene waited for the call to go through and then made his way up to the apartment where his sister was staying. They greeted each other happily.

"You're using my bedroom for the night," Janice said. "I'm sleeping on the couch in the living room."

Janice had taken up residence with her in-laws after her husband sailed to England with the 167th Ordinance Tire Repair Company. Gene had chuckled at the vision of his stylish, immaculate brother-in-law baking retread tires.

Rose, Janice's mother-in-law, ordered a hearty dinner from the hotel dining room, and the evening was spent in family small talk. The impending dangers of warfare were left undiscussed, a void that had to be filled with humorous chatter. A simultaneous silence occurred when the unsaid overwhelmed the trivia.

It was broken by Janice's father-in-law, Milton, a dapper and indirect gentleman. "Where are you heading?"

"We don't know yet," Gene lied. "We open our orders after we leave Newcastle."

Gene knew he was not permitted to divulge his destination. The crew had already opened the secret envelope halfway between Savannah and Newcastle, in compliance with orders. And there it was. Presque Isle, Maine; Gander Lake, Newfoundland; Greenland; Iceland; Prestwick, Scotland. Seeing those words written and stamped with the official Air Force seal thrust Gene from dream to reality like diving into ice cold water.

"You look tired," Milton said. "You better get some rest. Good luck and God bless."

"See you in the morning," said Janice. "Be sure to wake me before you leave."

Gene fell into a deep sleep, but the alarm clock buzzed in what seemed to be a few minutes. Four a.m.! Quietly, he showered and dressed.

He found Janice wrapped in her bathrobe, staring out the living room window. "I hardly slept a wink," she said. "Please take care of yourself. I'll count the days until you're back home safe and sound." With that, she gave Gene a tearful hug.

On the street, which was shrouded in the predawn shadows, Gene hurried toward the subway to shake off the chill air. He became acutely aware that this could be the last time he would ever walk this way or see his family again.

A lone cab cruised slowly toward him, and on impulse, he raised his hand to flag it.

"Where to?" asked the driver.

"Penn Station," said Gene with a sudden feeling of apprehension.

When he got to the train station, it was easy to spot Skipper at the gate in his patriotic outfit, and Gene's mood brightened as the puppy leaped and barked raucously to welcome him.

"How did he behave at your house?" Gene asked Al, who was there with the pup.

"Better than I did, I'm afraid. But I'm glad he was there. It was a… diversion."

"Yeah, I know what you mean."

* * *

At about 8:30 a.m. on March 8th, 1944, the crew gathered around their brand new B-17 Flying Fortress at New Castle Field. The shiny silver plane had been delivered to them at Hunter Field in Savannah.

Gene flushed with pride at the realization that he would be flying this graceful bomber, the culmination of the year of difficult training as an aviation cadet. He smiled to himself, remembering his obsession with model airplanes and his passion to place every part correctly. By the time he was twelve, his bedroom ceiling was covered with Piper Cubs, Aeroncas, Stimson Reliances, and Norsemans. He could still feel the thrill of their soaring wide circles, free as eagles until they glided to a soft landing in neighborhood parks.

"Let's take a walkthrough to satisfy ourselves that there aren't any problems before we leave for Presque Isle. It'll probably be easier to correct them here. You come too, Charlie," said J.O. Leonard, the first pilot, to Charles Bond, the crew's flight engineer.

Junie Oliver Leonard, Jr. was a native of Greenville, South Carolina. At age twenty-five, he was the oldest man in the crew and his steadiness was a stabilizing influence. Gene respected him as a person of impeccable character. Prematurely balding, he was jokingly called "Curly" by his fellow officers.

The nose of the plane, located below and forward of the cockpit, was the space shared by the bombardier and navigator. A chart table occupied the rear left side.

"Everything looks OK in here," said Charlie as he examined each of the two .50 caliber machine guns and the chin turret beneath the Plexiglas nose.

Gene climbed into the co-pilot's seat and carefully checked the operations of his flight controls and seat adjustments. J.O. did the same.

"Let's hope this big-ass bird gets us across the Atlantic," said J.O.

"From your mouth to God's ears."

Bob Stein, the navigator, made his way beneath Gene and J.O. down into the nose. "I suppose I don't have to worry too much about getting us lost between here and Presque Isle," he yelled.

"We'll risk it," Gene said. He liked Bob. The tall redhead was always ready with a humorous comment, and Gene felt relaxed in his presence. He admired Bob for interrupting his studies in optometry at Princeton to join the Air Corps. Imagining him as a future optometrist making jokes with his patients, Gene suddenly felt the chill of reality. He hoped there'd be a future, for all of them.

Shouldering past the top turret guns, located behind the cockpit, the group proceeded along the catwalk through the bomb bay and into the radio room, where Whitey Pearson was checking out his transmitters and receivers.

"Everything looks OK in here," said Charlie. Gene trusted the tall well-built Texan, whose expertise was valued by everyone. His job as an oil rigging mechanic prepared him well.

Behind the radio room, the ball turret gunner, left and right waist gunners, and tail gunner were busily checking their stations.

At that point, Al arrived, dragging Skipper forward on his leash. "Should we keep him on the navigator's table again?" Al asked Bob.

"Sure, sure, little dog. Just don't mess up my maps."

Up on the table, Skipper seemed as if he belonged. He sniffed the charts, kissed Bob's hand, rolled over to be scratched, and turned to find a comfortable spot, resting his head on his paws.

Skipper's golden jowls, eyebrows, and booties were a startling contrast to the overall shiny blackness of his coat, while his long fluffy ears appeared permanently waved. But most of all, there was a pleading expression in his eyes that said, "Take care of me!"

Gene hoped they could protect him through the trials that lay ahead, and patted Skipper's face. Skipper licked his fingers as if to say, "I trust you."

They fired up the engines, taxied around to the runway, and took off. Gene found himself breathing heavily at the stark awareness that this was the beginning of their entry into battle.

Thrilled by the New York skyline, and then comforted by the rolling New England hills, they landed at the Army Air Corps base in Presque Isle, Maine, their last stop before departing the U.S.A.

Gene had never been away from the States before and wondered what it would like living in a foreign country. Certainly there would be danger, but he had survived many unknowns during the Depression. He remembered leaving New York to work in Virginia at the Norfolk Navy Yard and how his family had warned him against going so far. Yet he needed the money, and knew that no one would be able to provide the sums to support him and his father, who was left devastated and unemployed after his wife died.

"Let's go, little dog. We both need to stretch our legs," said Bob as they exited from the nose of the plane. Gene chuckled watching Skipper prance in circles and wind his leash around Bob's ankles.

A truck provided transportation to the terminal, where they were assigned billets for the night. No one seemed to notice Skipper.

The barracks, uninviting and carelessly nailed together, were a far cry from the officers' quarters at Hunter Field in Savannah, and Gene wondered what life in a war atmosphere would be like.

He stretched out on the cot with Skipper busily jumping back and forth between each of his buddies. It had been just three months ago at the replacement depot in Salt Lake City that he found his name on a list of ten airmen. It didn't take long for him to realize that each of the men, a few of whom were still in their late teens, would grow to be an important part of his life.

Early the following morning they headed to the operations shack near the flight line for a briefing on the next leg of their trip to Gander, Newfoundland.

There in bold black letters was a sign that struck fear into Gene's heart. He made eye contact with Al, who stared back at him with raised brows. J.O. put his hand to his head.

"NO PETS ARE PERMITTED ABOARD
PLANES DEPARTING THE U.S.A."

"Now what do we do?" asked Bob.

"We'll have to take our chances," said Al. "We don't have any other choice."

"We need this like two extra holes in our heads!" said Bob.

Gene sensed trouble brewing. They'd have to figure out a strategy for dealing with Skipper during the rest of the flights.

They departed Presque Isle, and landed approximately three-and-a-half hours later amid mountainous banks of snow at Gander Airport.

"I feel like we're at the North Pole," said Gene, surveying the treeless terrain. He scanned the barren, craggy landscape and wondered what would convince anyone to live here. His face stung with the frozen spray, completing the dismal picture.

At the terminal, they were greeted by another sign.

"PERSONNEL CARRYING PETS ABOARD DEPARTING AIRCRAFT ARE SUBJECT TO COURT MARTIAL."

"You men will have to get rid of that dog," said the officer in charge. "You can take him to the Red Cross shack, and they'll see to it that he'll be sent home."

Lead footed and heavy hearted, Gene followed the others to the Red Cross in an adjacent building.

A young woman with the largest blue eyes Gene had ever seen stared at the little dog with the Air Force patches on his sweater. "What can I do for you?" she asked.

"We were told that you would ship our dog back to my

home in South Carolina. We're just sick about it, but I guess there's no way we can get around it. If you'll lend me a pen, I'll jot down my sister's address," said J.O., lifting Skipper onto the counter.

Skipper rolled over to have his tummy scratched. The Red Cross attendant reached to pat his head but stopped short. Instead, she searched each of their faces with her bright blue eyes. Gene didn't know what she saw, but it was all he could do to hide his emotions.

"Look, fellas. Nobody sends the pets home. After the planes depart, they simply take them out and shoot them."

Gene snatched Skipper off the counter and hid him inside his bomber jacket. The four of them hurried out the exit and returned to their overnight quarters.

"Court martial is no joke," said J.O. "Some heroes we'd be, grounded or demoted over a dog."

Gene's thoughts raced ahead. They had just completed the second leg of their flight, and already there were complications with Skipper. He wondered if it might be best to find a home for him with one of the G.I.s stationed at Gander. Problems like this had never occurred to him on that sunny December day in Avon Park, Florida.

"I was going to bring you guys a rabbit's foot," J.O.'s sister had said, presenting them with a round-bellied puppy. "But I decided that a real live good luck charm would be better. So here's your crew mascot. All he needs is a name."

Gene cleared his head. "We'll just have to keep him hidden until we get to Scotland. We can't leave him in this godforsaken place to be shot."

"Somehow we'll manage. I'm willing to risk it," said Bob.

The following morning, the crew assembled in a briefing room, where a film was shown depicting the approaches to the Greenland Air Base. "This ain't gonna be easy," whispered J.O., as he watched Bob taking copious notes on the maze of fjords and canyons.

The gray day promised change, and Gene hoped that the sun would prevail. While the officers plodded through the snow to check the weather, the rest of the crew set out toward the plane. Gene exhaled little puffs of fog into the frigid air, and he was glad to enter the warm operation's shack.

"You can expect a few snowstorms," warned the weather officer, raising his bushy eyebrows. "It's unpredictable near the Arctic Circle. Yup, you'll surely get some intermittent squalls." He smiled as if they were about to have a great adventure.

Back at the barracks, Gene called the dog. "C'mere, little guy," he said. "Don't make any noise!" Unzipping the bomber jacket, he tucked the dog into the warm fleece lining. Gene leaned forward to minimize the bulge and hoped no one would notice his stowaway.

Once in the air, Bob gave Gene and J.O. a northeasterly heading toward Greenland, and they were on their way, climbing into a threatening sky over the Atlantic Ocean.

At six thousand feet and fifteen minutes into the flight, Gene said to J.O., "Here's the snow the weather guy warned us about." A few flakes streamed past the cockpit windows, and it wasn't long before the flurries became a heavy snowfall. "Hey, J.O., there's some ice starting to build up on our wings. We better try to climb out of this mess."

"Yeah. If we can't get rid of the snow, at least a lower temperature might stop the ice from building up."

But as they reached ten thousand feet, the ice was still accumulating, and Gene tried calling the crew on the intercom. "Co-pilot to crew. Over. Co-pilot to crew. Over."

No one answered.

"What a bunch of jackasses. None of them have their headsets connected," Gene said, climbing out of his seat.

He yelled down into the nose for Al and Bob to put on their oxygen masks and then went back to the radio room, where the rest of the crew had gathered.

"Everyone, get back to your positions and plug in your oxygen masks. We're going to be at high altitude for awhile."

Although it was midday, the heavy clouds and blinding snow created a nighttime atmosphere, and Gene kept a cautious eye on the thickening ice. "Standard procedure is to turn on the de-icer boots only after a build-up of at least half an inch. It looks like we've got more than that now."

"Yeah," said J.O. "Let's give the boots a try."

With a prayer, Gene flicked the de-icer switch. As the boots started to bulge in and out, frozen chunks broke loose from the wings, banging against the plane like a passage from the "Anvil Chorus."

"Thank God," Gene said. "Now all we've got to do is climb out of this snow."

Finally, with the altimeter reading twenty-six thousand feet, the fortress popped out of the clouds into the clear blue sky. Gene breathed a sigh of relief.

He thought back to his first flight instructor, Jim Hanley, who had held his head in amazement when he discovered that Gene had never learned how to drive a car, which was typical for those who had grown up in the city like Gene. "Look what they sent me—a New York plumber!" Jim had exclaimed at his first lesson.

Gene was thankful that he was given a chance to fly and had been very proud when Mr. Hanley had come up to him at graduation and said, "You're going to be a good pilot, Hackel." Thinking back to his pilot training, Gene was suddenly struck with the realization that the little dog was in the plane with them.

"My God, J.O.! *Skipper!* I completely forgot. We've been up here for over an hour. I'm sick! He couldn't have survived this long without oxygen."

J.O. called on the intercom. "Pilot to bombardier or navigator. Over."

No response.

"I'm heartbroken, Gene," said J.O. "How could we have been stupid enough to bring him with us? It's all my fault."

Gene sat with a lump in his throat, tears welling up in his eyes. "Don't blame yourself, J.O. We're all guilty."

An hour later, Gene noticed the clouds breaking up, and he was able to spot patches of ocean indicating they had passed the storm.

Gene thought of Bob and Al down there in the nose with Skipper, helpless as they watched him go to sleep forever. He could imagine his lifeless body lying on the navigator's table and the pain his two crewmates must be feeling.

J.O. nosed the plane downward through an opening in the clouds.

At twelve thousand feet, Gene unplugged his oxygen mask, and with a sense of dread, climbed down the passageway into the nose of the plane. There, on the navigator's table, a delighted, frantic, tail-wagging Skipper leaped into the arms of an astonished Gene and vigorously washed his face with his tongue. Al and Bob sat smiling from ear to ear.

For a moment, he stood speechless, his throat tied in knots of joy. "How in the hell did he survive up there for over two hours without oxygen?"

"He wasn't without oxygen," Al said. "I spent the whole time sharing my mask with him. I took a breath, then I squeezed the mask over his snout. But I could see by the indicator that the little bastard wouldn't breathe. So I blasted the oxygen up his nose with the emergency valve."

"You're some peck of trouble, Skipper. We never know what's next with you, do we?" Gene wouldn't have cared if the peck increased to a bushel. He loved the little puppy with all his heart.

A quick check at the oxygen gauge showed that Al had almost drained the plane's supply to keep Skipper alive. But there was enough, and the dog had made it.

Navigating through the narrow fjords, thanks to Bob's notes at the briefing, Gene and J.O. were able to land them safely at the airbase.

Gene debarked the plane and surveyed the formidable, frozen mountains rising into the sky at both sides of the airfield. "Hope we don't have any trouble getting out of here. It looks pretty scary!"

"It sure does," said Bob. "That ice cap averages ten thousand feet high, and it'll take us over an hour to fly across it. One helluva place for a forced landing."

"God forbid," said Gene. "If you have any other pleasant thoughts like that, please keep them to yourself. Let's see where they're going to put us up for the night."

A stocky, red-faced truck driver gave a questioning glance at Skipper, but made no comment. They took a quick ride back to the barracks, happy to be safe and sound. It was a quiet afternoon, and the crew settled in to relax on their cots after the anxiety of the trip.

Skipper, on the other hand, was full of energy after his ordeal with the oxygen mask. From the corner of his eye, Gene caught the image of a shiny black fluff ball standing on his hind legs at the foot of Al's bed. Then he disappeared beneath it.

"What's that racket?" asked Al.

"I think it's Skipper playing with something under your bed," said Gene.

Skipper growled and made some smacking noises. No one made a move for a few minutes. Then gagging sounds followed by coughing aroused Al's curiosity. He hopped off his bed, dropped to his knees, and dragged Skipper out by his front paws.

"You little stinker!" shouted Al.

Gene sat upright and roared with laughter as Al held up his mangled leather flight helmet covered with a slimy coat of saliva.

"You good-for-nothing mutt. Is this the thanks I get for saving your life?"

At 6:00 a.m., the Charge of Quarters came in to rouse everyone. Skipper was tucked safely beneath the covers of Al's cot. Even though no one had said anything about him on their arrival, they felt safer keeping him out of sight.

When the group reached the operations shack for a weather briefing, Gene had Skipper hidden beneath his bomber jacket once again. They filed their flight plan with the officer in charge and were faced with another large sign on the wall, which read:

"PETS FOUND ABOARD PLANES LANDING IN ICELAND WILL BE DESTROYED UPON ARRIVAL."

"Well so far, with all the warnings since Presque Isle, you've made it, you goofy little guy," said Bob, scratching Skipper's ears.

"It's unthinkable for us to lose you now," J.O. added.

Settling into his co-pilot's seat, Gene wondered how they would deal with Skipper when they arrived in Iceland. He'd always been good at anticipating problems, but it seemed impossible to mentally write a script with one or more solutions to protect their mascot.

"You've got a worried look on your face, Gene. What's bugging you?" asked J.O., turning the plane onto the runway in preparation for takeoff.

"That sign got to me. Destroyed on arrival. It was like a stab in the heart!"

"I'm worried too, but there's nothing we can do about it now. I know we'll come up with something."

Gene hoped that J.O.'s "something" would save Skipper's life. What a crazy world! Fighting for democracy didn't seem to include the companionship of a small helpless puppy.

His thoughts were distracted by the two-mile-high ice cap, an eerie phenomenon. Gene remembered someone explaining that the famous icebergs, found floating in the waters below, were chunks broken from the mountainous glaciers, threatening ships at sea.

Out over the ocean, leaving the ice cap behind, Gene heard barking from below. "I'll be right back, J.O. I want to see what's going on."

Skipper, with his head held high, was standing on the chart table, yapping a chorus of triple notes, the meaning of which was a mystery to Gene.

"What's all the ruckus?" he asked.

"We're teaching him how to speak for treats," Bob said.

"For God's sake. What are you doing that for? We want him mute and invisible. Are you crazy? You'll get him shot!"

"Don't worry," Bob answered. "Every time we give him a treat and then say 'Speak!' along with hand signals to bark, he jumps in our laps."

"That's really great," said Gene, twisting his mouth in annoyance. "Now he's barking all the time!"

"Nah, he's just mad because I called him a bad boy when he took a leak on my maps."

The mystery was solved. "Look at these two big fools

squawking at me with biscuits in their hands!" Skipper seemed to be saying.

Luckily, Skipper never learned the trick, and the flight was uneventful except for periodic updates over the intercom.

Gene called the Iceland tower for landing instructions and was advised on which runway to use. Once on the ground, they were given taxi instructions and ordered to remain on board until the inspection officer completed his examination for pets.

"What are we going to do with Skipper?"

"I knew this would happen!"

"Oh, God, they'll kill him if they find him!"

A deadly silence hung over the plane.

"Let's put Skipper down in the camera hatch under the radio room floor!" shouted Charlie Bond.

"We all better say our prayers for him," Gene said, climbing back to the cockpit.

"It'll be freezing cold," Al said, offering the quilted cover of his Norden bombsight to keep Skipper warm.

Whitey Pearson yanked the panel out of the floor, and in one continuous motion, Al wrapped a confused, frightened Skipper in the bombsight cover, lowering him into the empty hatch.

"Be a good boy, Skipper. You'll be out in a few minutes," Al said. Whitey quickly replaced the floor panel.

A canvas-covered truck pulled up alongside the plane and a barrel-chested lieutenant, wearing a green parka and clumsy overshoes, climbed aboard. "Welcome to the Land of Lava-rock and Fishheads," he said. "Do you have any pets aboard?"

"No, sir," answered J.O. "Just the ten of us."

"I'll take a quick walkthrough." The lieutenant squeezed past the cockpit down into the nose. He searched beneath the navigator's table and behind the ammunition canisters. Fortunately, Al had stuffed Skipper's squeaky toys and leash into his pockets.

Finding nothing of import, the officer entered the radio room, stomping heavily across the floorboards. Gene was certain that his heart had stopped beating, for he was unable to breathe. *Please, dear God,* he thought, *don't let Skipper bark or whimper.*

The lieutenant began displacing the duffel bags piled around the room. He sniffed the air, and Gene hoped he wouldn't detect a trace of dog food odor wafting from the trash bag stowed in the corner.

"I've found all sorts of pets, from kittens to hamsters, hidden among baggage like this."

Gene remained standing on the panel over the camera hatch, anxiously awaiting the departure of the inspector, who then proceeded into the aft of the plane with Gene and J.O. following.

Eddie Metcalf sat in his ball turret, rotating it from side to side as if his life depended on it. Nutter and DeFudis, the waist gunners, stood wiping down the barrels of their guns, avoiding eye contact.

"Okay, men. I'm finished. You and your crew can unload your baggage now and get aboard my truck. I'll drive you to the terminal, where you can check in."

Gene looked at J.O., who shrugged in quiet frustration.

It was obvious that they had to leave the plane with Skipper submerged in the dark camera hatch.

That night in the barracks, they sat on the edges of their cots, while outside the swirling snow danced to the tune of a howling wind, reflecting Gene's macabre mood.

"Poor dog," Bob said. "Out there in the camera hatch. He must be freezing cold and scared to death, wondering where we are."

"For God's sake," Gene replied, "you don't have to make us feel worse than we already do."

"He'll be all right," countered Al. "We wrapped him in a quilt."

"The quilt won't help that sissy. He'll die from a heart attack," said J.O.

Gene pulled on his pants and fleece-lined bomber jacket. "I'm going out to the flight line to get him. We can't leave him out there all night."

"How in the hell are you going to find the flight line? You don't have a clue where it is," objected Bob.

"I'll go with you, Gene, and somehow we'll find our way to the plane," Al said.

The blackness, punctuated by the blowing snow, looked like a photo negative of a Van Gogh painting. In these conditions, it was hard to focus on a particular direction.

"How will we find the flight line?" asked Gene, already ankle deep in snow.

"God only knows," answered Al. "Let's just start walking down the road."

Minutes into their journey, a Jeep appeared, and the driver came to a halt. "Can I give you guys a lift? Where are you heading?"

"We want to get out to the flight line where our plane is parked," said Al as he and Gene climbed into the Jeep.

"The best direction I can give you is that our plane is near a large hangar alongside a couple of gasoline trucks," said Gene.

Fortunately, the driver had a thorough knowledge of the air base and brought them to the area where their plane was parked.

With the aid of a flashlight borrowed from the driver, they hurried to the radio room. Sounds of frantic scuffling and whimpering assured the two worried officers that Skipper was alive.

Lifting the quilted cover, they exposed a dazed, shivering dog. Gene's heart went out to the puppy as he clutched him to his chest. "Poor boy. Poor little fella. You'll be all right. You'll be OK" As if to forgive him, Skipper licked Gene's face, though he was still trembling from head to tail.

Hiding Skipper in his jacket, Gene climbed into the Jeep again, and the driver returned them to their Nissen hut, a half-cylinder corrugated steel structure designed as a military shelter. Despite its Spartan appearance, Gene welcomed the security and warmth it provided.

Bob and J.O. were euphoric. "You didn't think we'd leave you out there all alone in the camera hatch, did you?" said J.O., planting kisses on each of Skipper's ears.

Bob lifted him from J.O.'s cot. Skipper narrowed his eyes as if to say, "Poor me. Keep apologizing."

"Look at the little actor. He's eating it all up. OK, OK, we'll recommend you for the Distinguished Doggie Cross," said Bob.

"You came through like a real trooper," said Al.

Responding to their praises, Skipper waggled his rump and rushed back and forth between each of his friends.

"Maybe the lucky breaks we've had with Skipper's problems are a good omen for what we're facing down the road," said Gene.

"Amen," said J.O.

CHAPTER TWO

Skipper Joins the 385ᵗʰ

Prestwick was an enormous, sprawling airport for all planes arriving from the United States and Canada. J.O. was advised that they would spend a few days here before being given their Bomb Group assignment.

On the following morning, Gene and Al walked with Skipper to the Post Exchange, located almost a mile from where they were billeted. Gene no longer felt apprehension or the need to hide Skipper, who trotted along in a spirit of adventure.

"Hey! Sure feels good to take Skipper out for a walk in public."

"Yeah! It was a pain in the neck hiding him inside my jacket. It still stinks from doggy breath," said Gene.

From out of nowhere, a military official's sedan stopped abruptly alongside them, and an impeccably attired middle-aged officer exited from the back seat. Noting the eagles on his shoulders, Gene and Al promptly saluted.

"Where did you get that dog, Lieutenants?"

"South Carolina, sir," responded Al.

"Well, he's going to have to be quarantined here at the base infirmary for six months," growled the colonel.

"We don't expect to be here that long, sir," said Gene.

"It makes no difference how long you are or aren't going to be here in the U.K. Your dog is going to be impounded for six months." The colonel's voice escalated from annoyance to impatience. "They haven't had a case of rabies in the United Kingdom for over a hundred years, and we must respect their rules and regulations."

"How do we find the infirmary?" asked Al.

The colonel gave very clear directions and returned to his vehicle.

"Now what the heck are we going to do?" asked Gene.

Skipper squatted to pee.

"C'mon, little fella. Let's go. We're in this together," said Gene.

On the walk back to the billets, hiding Skipper didn't occur to Gene. It wasn't likely that he would come upon the colonel again in this vast military complex, but just as they were about to enter the barracks compound, Al muttered under his breath, "Look who's coming!"

Gene turned, and to his astonishment, the colonel's command car stopped once again.

Red in the face, the colonel shouted, "I thought I told the two of you to take that dog to the infirmary!"

"I'm sorry, sir," said Al, "but we just weren't able to find it. We were planning to look once again after lunch."

The colonel repeated his directions and cautioned, "The two of you better see to it that this is done without any further delay."

They nodded without saying anything, and headed off, hoping for the best.

J.O. and Bob were waiting for them at the barracks with the word that the crew had been assigned to the 385th Bomb Group and they were to fly their B-17 to the base at Great Ashfield the following morning.

It was welcome news to Gene, who had decided to avoid any further confrontation with the base's commanding officer.

"You're about to go on the final leg of your journey, Skipper. After tomorrow, you shouldn't have any more problems," said Gene.

"His may be over, but ours are just beginning," J.O. added.

Happily, they didn't encounter the colonel again before leaving in the morning, and soon were on their way to their next destination. The Great Ashfield air base, home of the 385th, was situated in the middle of a large farm in East Anglia. Individual planes were distributed over wide areas, parked on circular concrete "hardstands." Noting their placement, J.O. commented, "It sure minimizes the risk of being destroyed in a German bomber attack."

They were welcomed to the 550th Bomb Squadron by Lieutenant Colonel Bill Tesla and the squadron executive officer, Captain Ed Stern, who showed them to the officers' barracks they would occupy.

Afraid to disclose Skipper's presence, Gene had him hidden in his loosely unzipped bomber jacket. As they walked inside their new barracks, Captain Stern tapped Gene on his shoulder, smiling. "What've you got on the other end of that leash trailing on the ground behind you?"

Gene froze. Obviously caught, he opened his bomber jacket and introduced Skipper to the delighted Captain, who was not one bit concerned at his arrival.

Captain Stern showed them the four cots they would occupy and explained, "You'll be pleased to meet the other three crews. They should be returning from a bombing mission in a couple of hours. At 8:00 tomorrow morning, you'll report to the Briefing Room on the flight line to receive indoctrination."

"How're we going to keep Skipper from peeing on some other guy's bed?" asked Bob after Captain Stern left their barracks.

Gene remembered only too well those unpleasant past occurrences back in Florida. "Let's put his bowls for food and water between my bed and J.O.'s. That might do the trick."

"It better work, or we'll have twelve more enemies in addition to the Luftwaffe," said Bob.

Gene sprawled on his cot after unpacking, and Skipper leaped up to join him.

The rumble of a truck, followed by squealing brakes, prompted him to look out the window, where he saw a group of men jumping off the tailgate. The 550th Bomb

Squadron had returned from its mission. "Woof, woof," barked Skipper, as the exuberant group burst into the barracks.

A tall, dark-haired young man wearing bombardier wings said, "How about this? We're going to have a canine bunkmate!" Extending his hand to Gene, he added, "My name is John Demereaux." The other men introduced themselves, warmly welcoming the four new arrivals.

"How did it go up there today?" J.O. asked.

"Not too bad," responded one of the pilots. "The 549th lost one of its planes. The rest of us picked up some flak damage."

Gene was taken aback by the lieutenant's casual attitude regarding the loss of a crew. He wondered if this was typical but was afraid to ask.

John Demereaux sat down on his cot, and Skipper promptly jumped into his lap. "You're going to be good company," he said to Skipper. "Where did he come from?"

"South Carolina," said Gene. "And don't ask what we went through getting him here!"

That evening on the chow line in the mess hall, Bob whispered to Gene, "Look at the portions they're dishing out. It's not enough to share with Skipper."

When it was Gene's turn, he said to the K.P., "I'm really hungry. Can I have a little more Spam?"

The K.P. slapped two extra slices on his plate. As he moved along, repeating the request, the last of the servers looked at his tray piled high with food, and with a grin said, "Hearty appetite, Lieutenant."

"This is going to be a hassle," complained Gene, spooning Skipper's portion into the mess kit.

That night, Gene jotted a note to Janice.

Dear Jan,

Well, here we are at our Bomber Base in the U.K. Our flight from the U.S.A. to England was a nightmare because of problems with Skipper. He nearly got shot, we had to force feed him oxygen at high altitudes, and he almost froze to death in the plane's camera hatch. To top that, they wanted to quarantine him for six months.

Feeding him is a pain in the neck, and each night we all have to contribute parts of our supper for his daily meal. Too bad there's no place for us to buy regular dog food.

Hope all is well with Milton and Rose. What do you hear from Reggie? I'd love to find him here in England. Wish me luck.

Much love,
Gene

Indoctrination briefing the following morning was a sobering experience for Gene. Four replacement crews, totaling forty men, were seated in the Ready Room, a theater-like setting. The first officer to speak was from the Intelligence section. He spoke in a stoic monotone. "Current statistics here at the 385th show that only three out of ten bomber crews survive twenty-five missions. Flying a close formation is key to improving your chances. You must fly tight enough to prevent enemy fighters from flying through your formation. This forces them to pass above or below you, which will afford maximum fire power."

He went on to relate in detail how everyone was to function with the French underground. "If you have to bail out or crash-land in France, the French will rush to the scene to beat out the Germans. They will take you to a safe house, where you'll be carefully interrogated. Don't be surprised if they include questions about baseball stars and comic strip characters, which only Americans can easily answer.

"The first thing you must do is bury your parachutes. Be sure to hold on to your escape kits, which will be issued to you after passport photos are taken of you dressed in European-style civilian clothes collected for this purpose. The kit also contains maps and concentrated survival food. This will be your lifeline. It's vital to exercise daily in order to condition yourself for the possible hike over the Pyrenees into Spain. Do exactly as you're told. Your lives will be in French hands. Their safety will be in yours, so keep all your discussions secret. If you come down in Germany, lotsa luck!"

A second officer followed with a description of how the flight formations were arranged and advised the newcomers that they would be flying Tail-End-Charlie for the first few missions until they gained combat experience.

"Starting tomorrow morning, each crew will be separated for your first two missions. You will be assigned to fly with crews who have had fifteen or more combat sorties under their belts. This will give you a chance to acclimatize your-selves to antiaircraft fire and possible German fighter attacks. Trucks will drive you to the mess hall for breakfast and then on to the Ready Room out on the flight line. The length of our missions vary anywhere from five to nine hours.

"I cannot overemphasize the importance of keeping your-self in good physical condition. Many hours at high altitude is demanding, so get plenty of sleep. I wish you all the best!"

After the briefing ended, Al was the first to speak. "Three out of ten—that's a helluva set of numbers. It's hard for me to believe it's that bad."

"Maybe they're exaggerating," said Bob.

"Whatever," Gene commented. "It's a grim prospect."

"I'm not looking forward to being separated for the first two missions," said J.O. "I'll feel better when our whole crew is together."

"I don't like this Tail-End-Charlie bit either," said Bob. "Seems like we could easily be picked off by German fight-ers."

Gene wondered how he would react to exploding shells and fighter attacks. It was impossible to imagine. Then he turned off all the negative scenarios. "If all the rest of these guys face up to it every day, we will too!"

The long walk to the 550th Squadron area helped clear Gene's mind. Then he caught sight of Skipper straining at his leash, which was wrapped around the door handle of their billet.

"Who the hell tied him out here?" questioned J.O., un-doing Skipper from his restraint.

The door opened and out stepped a Private First Class wearing a fatigue uniform, with a pistol, holster, and belt slung over his shoulder. He had a large broom in one hand and a trash can in the other. "Does dis pooch belong ta youse guys?" he asked in classic Brooklynese.

"Yes, he's ours," answered J.O. "And what's your name, Private?"

"All da guys call me Gat. It's easia ta rememba dan my real name," he said, patting his gun and holster.¬

Gene couldn't help smiling. There was something humorous and lovable about this big, square New Yorker.

"I'm sorry I had to tie yer pooch outside, but he kept bitin' da broom an' I couldn't get my woik done. What do youse call 'im?"

"His name is Skipper," answered Al.

"Hey, Skippa, you an' me are gonna be pals, cause you'll be seein' me every day." Turning to the officers, he explained his job as charge of quarters for the squadron. "I keep da place ship-shape, an' I wake youse guys before each mission."

"We have an extra job for you," said J.O. "That's if you're willing to do it."

"All depends on what it is. I'm listenin'," said Gat.

"It would be great when we're flying missions if you could find time to take Skipper for a walk in the middle of the day. We don't want him peeing all over the place. Also, could you make sure he has water in his bowl?"

"Shuah, shuah, I can do dat. I'll take him for a walk now." As Skipper toddled off with Gat, Gene had the impression that their mascot was being adopted by an amiable mobster.

Early the following morning, Gene felt a blast of cold air, followed by Gat's loud announcements of the officers' names who would be flying in the day's mission. They were to report to the Ready Room at 0600 hours. Gene squinted from the bright lights and looked at his watch. *Feels like I just hit the hay,* he thought, swinging his legs over the edge of his cot.

Skipper started prancing around their beds. He jumped from Gene to J.O. to Al to Bob as if to say, "I'm going with you!"

Gene's heart sank. Skipper would be spending his first day alone without them. *What a relief that Gat agreed to look after him,* he thought.

The target for the day was a munitions factory in the Ruhr Valley. Gene and Ray Leeds were assigned as co-pilot and tail gunner with Lieutenant Guyler, who had already completed twenty missions. J.O., Al, and Bob, along with the five enlisted men, were all similarly assigned to experienced crews. The mission would be approximately seven hours long, with Gene taking his turns at the controls.

As they got into the air and the formation approached the target area, Gene was startled by heavy barrages of exploding shells from German antiaircraft batteries. Despite chunks of shrapnel pounding through the plane, he was amazed at the casual coolness displayed by Lieutenant Guyler, who made it appear commonplace.

Suddenly, a string of bombs dropped from the lead plane as the group's commanding officer called, "Bombs Away!" In unison, the entire formation released their loads of high explosives, raining death and destruction on the factory buildings below. The whole complex appeared to lift and then collapse amidst billows of black and orange smoke.

"Let's get the hell out of here!" called Colonel Tesla. The massive formation of fortresses pivoted in a tight turn away from the target, and as Gene looked down, he saw the entire area of devastation. With a great sense of relief, he realized that they had completed their first mission.

Skipper greeted them on their return to the billets.

"We made it, little fella. No losses. Mission One. You're our good luck charm." Gene swept him up into his arms and let Skipper's pink tongue kiss his chin and nose.

Mission Two would be a different story.

The next morning, Gene joined Ray Leeds at the hardstand where Lieutenant Guyler's B-17 was parked.

"Gosh, Lieutenant, this is gonna be a long one," Gene said.

Their target was the complex of aircraft factories at Warnemunde on the Baltic Sea, a place Hermann Goering thought would be safe from attack by Allied planes.

Ray furrowed his brow. Usually easygoing, he appeared somber and apprehensive.

Gene sensed his uneasiness and said, "Let's get through this one today, Ray, and tomorrow the ten of us will be back together again."

The flight to Warnemunde seemed interminable, made more so by their need to circumnavigate the antiaircraft positions reported by the Allied espionage units. At twenty-eight thousand feet, Gene was impressed with the ordinary appearance of Warnemunde. It could be Akron, Albany, or Chattanooga.

As the formation started its bomb run toward the factories, all hell broke loose. Black clouds of exploding antiaircraft shells erupted with flak so thick you could walk on it.

Abruptly, their plane was pounded by a shell that exploded between the open bomb bay doors.

"Radio to crew. I'm hit! I'm hit!" screamed the radio operator. "And the radio room's on fire!"

"Tail gunner to crew. Somebody come back and help me!" cried Ray Leeds. "My leg is smashed."

Gene could hear the desperation in his voice and called on the intercom, "Who has a portable oxygen bottle?"

"I've got one!" replied Bill Shannon, the navigator, as he scrambled from the nose of the plane back to the radio room.

Within seconds, Gene got another report from Shannon on the intercom. "I beat the fire out with my jacket. The boxes of chaff were burning. The radio operator looks okay—just a bad cut on his forehead. Blood is running into his eyes. The whole bomb bay and radio room are full of holes. I'm on my way back to help the tail gunner." All this was spit out in a rapid-fire stream of sentences.

With bursting shells continuing to pummel their airplane, Gene's eyes were glued on the lead plane with its gaping bomb bay. *Drop those damn bombs already,* he thought. His impatience was intense, and the wait felt like an eternity.

At last, the "Bombs Away" order came from the group leader, and the formation started their turn away from the target.

"Bombardier to Pilot. Our bombs didn't release! The salvo handle isn't working."

"Pilot to Bombardier. Keep working that handle. The bombs may not be secure, and they could let loose when we land."

"Shannon to crew. Ray is flailing about in pain. I've dragged him from the tail to the waist. I'm using my belt as a tourniquet, and I strapped an oxygen mask to his face."

"Co-pilot to Navigator. Grab a first-aid kit and get some morphine injected into him as fast as you can."

"Shannon to Co-pilot. I gave Leeds the shot of morphine and he's still thrashing around and trying to pull off his oxygen mask. Now he's gagging and might throw up."

"Co-pilot to Pilot. If we don't drop down to breathable air, Ray might not make it."

"Pilot to crew. If we leave the formation, we could invite an attack by enemy fighters. Any objections?"

The okay came through loud and clear. Guyler eased the plane downward. Fortunately there was a cloud layer which provided a safety cover.

How many things can go wrong in a matter of seconds? Gene reflected. *What a terrific crew! They were ready to risk their lives to help one man, someone they didn't even know two days ago. Now here we are with all our lives at stake if we can't dump these twelve five-hundred-pound bombs.*

"Pilot to crew. You can get rid of your oxygen masks now. We're at ten thousand feet."

Guyler turned to Gene. "We've got a tough decision to make. There's no way I'm going to attempt landing this plane

38

with the bombs aboard. We'll give it some time, and then we'll radio Great Ashfield for permission to turn on the automatic pilot before we reach the English coast and bail out. We can let the plane crash into the channel."

Gene nodded. "Let's hope we don't have to do it."

"Take the controls, Gene. I want to go back and have a look-see at the damage and Leeds' condition."

Gene guided the plane westward toward England. He told Shannon to get back to his navigator's table. "We need to have a fix on where we are," he said. "I'll duck down below the clouds so you can pinpoint our position."

It took Shannon a few minutes to give Gene a new compass heading.

Guyler returned to the cockpit with a grave expression on his face. "Leeds' leg is a mess. It looks like it might be severed a couple of inches below the knee. I hope they'll be able to save it."

Gene noticed that the clouds which had provided cover were starting to break up. "If we lose them, we'll be sitting ducks for an enemy fighter attack," he cautioned.

"I agree. We're nowhere near the French coast, and at this altitude we'll be picked up by German radar," said Guyler.

"Pilot to crew. We're going to drop down as close as possible to ground level. It'll be choppy, so stay seated and watch out for enemy planes."

"Bombardier to crew. I think I figured out why the bombs won't salvo. The doors buckled when that shell exploded. They need to be completely open for them to let go. I'm going to keep working the doors."

Gene didn't relish the idea of bailing out and hoped the bombardier would save the day.

A short time later an excited voice yelled, "Bombs Away." The plane lifted as the lethal load dropped, exploding harmlessly on empty pasture land below. Gene breathed a sigh of relief. *Now all we need to do is make it to the French coast without being picked off by enemy planes.*

Crossing the English channel, they welcomed the sight of the White Cliffs of Dover. Gene called the Great Ashfield tower, advising them of Leeds' condition, and requested an ambulance, which was waiting for them as they turned off the runway. Minutes later, Ray was rushed to an off-base military hospital.

Gene ignored Skipper's customary welcome when he returned to his quarters. The other planes had not landed, and he was glad to be alone.

He reviewed the events of the last eight hours: heavy barrages of flak, an almost direct hit, fire in the radio room, Ray Leeds calamitous wound, a threat of unreleased bombs exploding on landing. He thought, *My God, this was just the second mission, and we have twenty-three to go.*

Gene stretched out on his bed and closed his eyes. A wet, slimy rubber bone dropped on the back of his hand, an invitation from Skipper to play. "Please, Skipper, not now!"

The little dog hopped up on the cot, and with his head cocked to one side, peered into Gene's eyes. "I don't know what happened," he seemed to say, "but I'll help you get through all of this. You'll see. After all, you've still got me!"

With a sigh, Gene relented, grasped the sticky bone, and

tossed it across the room. Skipper leaped to the floor, scurried to retrieve it, and deposited it on the blanket. *How simple life can be,* thought Gene as Skipper opened a window to the joy of the moment.

He wished he could block out the image of Ray Leeds' severed leg. If only men were like dogs, with such uncomplicated goodness, these horrors would never happen.

Skipper snuggled up, resting his head on Gene's chest, as if he understood.

During the following few missions, they flew Tail-End-Charlie. It was no picnic, but it was comforting for Gene to be together with J.O. and the rest of the crew. Bob Moffet became the new tail gunner, and his cheerful demeanor diffused some of Gene's feelings of sorrow over Ray Leeds' unexpected misfortune.

When the crew completed its sixth mission, they went on a seventy-two-hour leave to London.

Gene was impressed with the blackout conditions planned with such care. Every entrance was constructed with double doors or mouse maze entryways in order to prevent any possible leakage of light.

Antiaircraft artillery emplacements, operated by young women, were strategically located throughout Hyde Park. The spirit of the British people was incredible, and Gene felt privileged to be among them.

After three days of respite from aerial combat, they returned to Great Ashfield and were shocked to learn that their plane, flown by another crew, had been shot down.

"It could've been us!" said Al.

"A helluva way to get a new plane!" added J.O.

Bob slumped on his cot. "What a way to end a three-day leave!"

The gloom was interrupted by the arrival of Gat and Skipper. "Hey, youse guys. I got three days woith of mail heah and a carton for Lieutenant Hackel. Skippa's all yours now. I've had it wid 'im."

Skipper pulled away, dragging his leash while greeting each of his pals. His entire rump was contorted in a euphoric shimmy of excitement.

Gene examined the box, hastily scanning the return address. "Oh, boy! It's from my sister. This is gonna be great! We'll have ourselves a feast on some goodies from home!"

Al, Bob, and J.O. were all smiles as they gathered around Gene.

Tearing at the wrapping, he salivated in anticipation of his sister's Toll House cookies, delicious chocolate walnut brownies, and assorted stateside candy.

Gene reached into the open box and pulled out the first item beneath the paper stuffing. "Oh look, she included something for Skipper." He held up a small box labeled Dog Yummies.

"How about that?" laughed J.O.

With both hands, Gene grasped a few more items: Milk Bones, Dog Treats, canned dog meat, and a paper package of Kibble. Gene dug his hands among the wads of paper, frantically searching for whatever treats his sister might have included for him. There were none.

"I'll be damned," said Bob.

"This is not to be believed," said Al as he surveyed the cot full of gourmet dog products.

Gene shook his head with disappointment and embarrassment. "She could have at least tucked in a couple of five-cent Hershey bars for her kid brother." He felt ridiculous.

Opening the box of Dog Yummies, Gene said with a touch of forced humor, "Here, Skipper. Look what Aunt Janice sent you."

Gene held out a small caramel-colored square between his fingers. Skipper rushed over for his handout and snatched the morsel.

After one chew he opened his mouth, stuck out his tongue, and with his tail between his legs, ejected the Yummy onto the floor between Gene's feet. "You ungrateful little son of a bitch," yelled Gene. "You're going to eat these treats if I have to shove them down your throat."

Lifting him up on his hind legs, Gene pried open Skipper's jaw and pushed a fresh Yummy into his mouth, squeezing his snout and holding it shut. Gene waited as Skipper obediently tolerated the unpleasant situation.

"Now, doesn't that taste good?" asked Gene, finally releasing his grip.

Skipper, his chops curled in a look of disgust, deposited the partially chewed, sticky dog candy onto Gene's lap.

J.O. rocked with laughter. "What do you expect of the poor dog? His meals have been the same as ours since he was eight weeks old. How would you like to try a dog Yummy?"

"No thanks. You've made your point. But my sister hasn't heard the end of this yet!"

CHAPTER THREE
Skipper: A Charm That Works

The target for their seventh mission would be the Messerschmitt aircraft factories in Augsburg, Bavaria, which were being defended by scores of 105 millimeter antiaircraft batteries.

"All of us better be wearing our flak vests on this mission," said J.O. "Sounds like we're gonna pick up some pretty brutal battle damage from all those 105s."

"Did they have to give us such a long one on our first day back? Nine hours is pretty rough," complained Bob.

The weather was crystal clear and they encountered no enemy action as the formations crossed France into Bavaria.

All at once, as they approached Augsburg, the sky blackened with terrifying gremlin-shaped explosions, followed by the boom, bang, rat-a-tat of shrapnel pounding through the entire length and breadth of the plane. Gene jolted forward as pieces of shrapnel slammed into the armor plating behind his seat, leaving him breathless for several seconds. It felt as though he had been pounded in the back with a sledgehammer.

"Bombardier to crew. Let's have a damage report. Over," Al called on the intercom.

Each crewmember reported extensive flak damage in their areas, but no one was wounded. The antiaircraft fire continued with punishing accuracy, and Gene was stunned at the sight of billowing parachutes bailing out of fortresses spiraling down in flames.

The "Bombs Away" call came across the intercom none too soon, and the traditional "Let's get the hell out of here" was music to his ears.

Before the formation could complete its turn off the target, J.O. grabbed his left shoulder and shouted, "Take the controls, Gene. I'm hit!"

"Where?" asked Gene with a tremor in his voice.

"My left arm, up near the shoulder," he answered, his eyes wide with fright.

Gene kept the plane in tight formation, glancing back and forth nervously at his wounded crewmate, whose forehead was now pale and wet. "Are you nauseous, J.O.?"

"Yes, I am. But I think I'll be all right."

The return flight across Bavaria was peppered with reports from each of the crewmembers describing the damage near their positions. *It's a miracle that all four engines are still running,* Gene thought, and he prayed that the plane would land without falling apart.

"Navigator to Pilot. We've just crossed the French border, J.O. We'll have you back at the base in a couple of hours. Just hang in there."

A formation of P-51 Mustang fighters approached to escort the bombers back to England.

"What a blessing to have their company," said Gene. "Now all we have to do is get this beat-up plane on the ground in one piece."

Circling Great Ashfield, Gene called the tower, requesting transportation to take J.O. to the infirmary. He flicked the switch to lower the landing gear, hoping it would function normally. Fortunately, the plane touched down softly onto the runway.

A Jeep waited for them on the perimeter strip. J.O. tore off his leather flight jacket and shirt in order to examine his wound. A small, dark metal chunk, the size of fingertip, pinged to the ground. "I want that!" said J.O., bending to retrieve his memento.

The Jeep sped off with a smiling, wounded pilot holding his trophy in the air between his thumb and forefinger.

Al looked up at the Plexiglass nose, shaking his head. "I guess it wasn't my time," he said, staring at the shattered and perforated bombardier's station.

"You guys tease us every time we load those three heavy sheets of armor plating into the nose before each mission," said Bob. "Maybe we should go steal another few pieces. It sure felt good to have something to crouch behind!"

"O.K., fellas. Let's get a quick assessment of the damage," said Gene. Each of the crewmembers did their own count and came up with an estimate of two hundred and sixty holes.

Al backed away from the plane and with a theatrical gesture, turned to Gene and said, "From this I make a living!"

During the debriefing session, an engineering officer informed the crew that their plane would have to be scrapped.

When they returned to their barracks, Gene smiled in anticipation of Skipper's joyous greeting. "Here, Skipper," he yelled, swinging the door open. "We're home!"

But there was no greeting, just silence.

"Where the hell is he?" asked Bob.

"Maybe he's asleep under one of the cots," said Al.

"That's ridiculous!" retorted Gene. "He's always awake and at the door when we get back from a mission. Oh, I know. Gat must have taken him for a walk."

At that moment, Gat, arms full of mail and packages, lumbered into the barracks. "I hoid we lost a few planes today," he said, casting his eyes toward the ceiling. "Shuah glad youse guys made it back!"

"We're glad too, but where's Skipper?" Gene asked. "He's not here and we thought he was with you."

Gat stiffened. "I left him heah when I brought him back from his walk around lunchtime. Maybe some of da other guys who weren't on da mission accidentally let him loose."

"For God's sake!" Gene said with alarm. "I hope he didn't run off and get lost."

"Wait a minute! I think I have an idea where he is," said Gat. "He may be in the enlisted men's barracks with Static."

"Static? Who's Static?" asked Bob.

"She's a little tan and white mutt dat belongs to one of da radio operators named Smitty. He lets her run loose all da time, and for da last eight or nine days, she's been walkin' wid us. I think Skippa has a crush on her."

"So what barracks is he in?" asked Al with a grin.

"Barracks Four. Let's go," said Gat, dumping his load of mail on the nearest cot.

They hurried toward the enlisted men's area, a few hundred yards down the road. In the space between Buildings Three and Four, Gene spied Skipper and Static frolicking and cavorting, yipping and yelping, in one big ball of fur, having the time of their lives. "Here, Skipper," he called.

Skipper looked toward Gene briefly but ignored the call.

Bob called again in a demanding voice. "Skipper, come over here right now, you bad boy!"

Skipper stopped and barked as if to say, "Bug off. I'm busy!"

"Come over here, I said!" Bob commanded, expecting obedience. Instead, Skipper resumed his playful defiance, ignoring Bob's order. "What's with him? He's never acted this way before."

"Are you kidding? We're interrupting his lovemaking," said Al.

"Well, that's enough. Come over here, Skipper!"

Skipper disengaged from Static, looked at Bob, and for a moment, it seemed he would obey. Instead, he blinked his eyes, trotted to the building's wall, and lifted his rear leg.

"I'll be damned!" shouted Al. "He finally became a man!"

It took a good fifteen minutes to corner Skipper and separate him from his lady friend.

J.O. was there to greet them on their return, a big smile on his face, a large bandage on his arm. "Here I am, your wounded pilot! I'm being recommended for a Purple Heart."

"They're getting pretty generous with the medals," joked Bob.

"Is that so?" J.O. turned to show an inflamed swelling the size of a baseball.

"You're lucky you only had one hole. They told us that our plane is beyond repair and they're scrapping it," Al said.

"What did you do with your Augsburg souvenir?" asked Gene.

"It's on our dresser. I'm going to have it framed."

Skipper jumped up on J.O., as if to say, "Hey! You need special attention!"

"Skipper has a girlfriend named Static," Al said.

"You're better off than we are, little fella." J.O. chuckled, pulling Skipper up beside him onto his cot.

Gene pulled his towel off their shared bureau. "I'm going to take a shower now. Maybe it'll wash this mission out of my head."

CLINK. CLANK. Something fell to the floor. Gene scanned the surface of the bureau. J.O.'s prize was no longer there. "J.O., I think my towel swept your hunk of shrapnel onto the floor," Gene said, kneeling on all fours.

J.O. bolted out of his cot and joined Gene. As they brushed their hands back and forth, Skipper, sensing a game, teamed up in the hunt with his two big friends.

He sniffed audibly shoulder to shoulder with the men, stepping on their hands, crawling under the bed, dragging out a sock, and offering it to J.O. as his contribution to the fun.

"Damn it, Skipper. Will you get out of our way?" J.O. shoved Skipper aside.

Skipper barked with joy, seeming to interpret J.O.'s tone as a call to action. He scrambled under the bureau, scratching and snorting, continuing his search for whatever.

Gene and J.O. covered the area, inch by inch, with their bare hands, which by now were covered with dirt and scratches from the coarse, unfinished plywood floor. Skipper emerged smacking his lips, with a strange look on his face and an unknown morsel in his mouth.

The two pilots stared in frustrated wonderment at the mysterious disappearance of J.O.'s trophy. "It's almost as if it evaporated into thin air," said J.O.

"More like swallowed up," said Gene. "Skipper, you little thief, did you eat J.O.'s piece of flak?"

The little dog tilted his head to the side.

The piece of flak was never found.

During the next several weeks, their targets included several cities, now battle famous. In raids from the Austrian border to the Baltic Sea and west to east from France to Poland, the 385th hit, and hit hard: Berlin, Nuremberg, Ludwigshafen, Magdeburg, Merseburg, Koblenz, Stuttgart, Aachen, Hanover, Wurzburg, and others whose German syllables spilled from Gene's tongue as if it were his native language.

His emotions were dulled by the appalling losses of men and planes, creating a protective shell of detached indifference to the daily statistics. It was only when crews who shared Gene's barracks failed to return that he felt a deep sadness and heartbreak.

Patterns of behavior and superstition evolved during these weeks. For example, Gene would never leave the barracks for the flight line without giving Skipper a hug and a kiss before departing.

Once, with an earlier than usual mission wake-up call, Gene hurried out to board the waiting truck, neglecting his regular goodbye routine. With a jolt of memory, he yelled, "Hold it, guys! I forgot something. I'll be right back." He leaped off the truck, rushed into the barracks, lifted his little friend, and planted a kiss on his head.

The other crewmembers acted out their own rituals with Skipper, although they never shared them with one another. Gene observed Al showing Peggy's picture to him, whispering something in his ear. One time he caught J.O. opening the door and holding Skipper up toward the sky. He couldn't figure what Bob was doing, but every morning before a mission, he would take his shaving kit and tuck the little dog under his arm, disappearing to the latrine.

It was obvious that Skipper had become the guardian angel of good luck and survival.

CHAPTER FOUR

Skipper's Misadventure

Early in May, the spring rains turned into frequent heavy downpours. The low-hanging cloud cover and damp barracks matched Gene's feelings of discomfort. Endless missions made it seem that the war would go on forever.

For five consecutive days, it rained without letting up, and the group struggled through the murky skies over Germany to find their targets. On the sixth morning, Gene was elated to hear the announcement that the mission would be scrubbed.

"How about some bridge at the officers' club?" asked Al, whose voice reflected the happiness of being rescued from a firing squad.

Gene declined the offer, saying he'd rather catch up on some correspondence. Skipper hopped up on his cot and cuddled against his hip. Removing a few sheets of V-Mail paper from his footlocker, Gene wrote:

May 6, 1944

Dear Dad,

I'm receiving mail from everybody now. I'm too tired to write a long letter. We're practically living in our airplanes. When Sherman said, "War is hell," he wasn't kidding. I've seen carnage in the air and on the ground. Up to date, I've flown eleven missions, otherwise nothing new. That's all for now so lots of love and write.

Gene

He dropped the letter into the outgoing mailbox alongside the barracks door. Writing a letter addressed only to his father reminded him that his mother was no longer alive. He imagined her hearing about the frightful losses of men and planes and how terrified she would have been.

Gene glanced at his watch. It was already ten o'clock. Skipper yelped with excitement, his way of asking to go for a walk. "C'mon, little fella. It stopped raining. Let's go get some fresh air."

Skipper had learned to follow along without a leash, which gave him more freedom to explore. Outside, the muggy air held the fragrance of spring vegetation mixed with the musty scent of farm animals.

"C'mon, Skipper. Let's go!" Gene shouted, clapping his hands. Skipper acted as if he didn't hear, obviously enamored with his hunting instincts.

The paved road leading from the barracks toward Squadron Headquarters was a strip of asphalt surrounded by two drainage ditches filled with thick, muddy water. Gene kept his eye on Skipper, who lagged behind. Turning the corner, he quickened his pace in order to get to the farm area where Skipper enjoyed romping in the fields.

"Let's go!" Gene repeated, looking over his shoulder at his little pal, who continued smelling the grasses lining the troughs. A whistle accompanied by hand gestures finally attracted Skipper's attention. He stopped in his tracks, appeared to assess the distance, took a few steps backward, and leaped diagonally across the corner of the ditch in what resembled a ballet jump.

"Oh, my God," Gene groaned as he watched him splash into the quagmire. He rushed to the spot where Skipper had disappeared, but he was nowhere to be seen. Without thinking, Gene immediately jumped into the knee-high water, his hands desperately searching the depths to rescue his friend. It was almost as if the mud had swallowed him up. Several seconds seemed like minutes before his hands felt Skipper's limp body.

In a single motion, he lifted the dog into the air and frantically struggled back up to the road. Holding Skipper by his back legs, Gene shook him up and down, dislodging clumps of mud and water from his throat. Skipper gasped and gagged. He was barely breathing.

A Jeep screeched to a halt, apparently sensing an emergency. "Can I help, Lieutenant?" asked a young sergeant wearing a peaked baseball cap and a fatigue uniform.

"I've got to get my dog to the infirmary! He almost drowned, and he's having trouble breathing! Would you drive me over there?"

"I'm sorry, Lieutenant, I've got a rush letter to deliver to Colonel Tesla, and I have to wait for an answer. Just take my Jeep and drive there yourself. I can wait here 'til you get back." He jumped out and hurried into the Administration Building.

Gene stood speechless. He couldn't bring himself to shout after the sergeant that he didn't know how to drive!

With his heart pounding, he climbed into the driver's seat, laying Skipper gently beside him. Now what? It was always a source of embarrassment that he had never learned to operate an automobile. Yet he had paid careful attention to drivers as they clutched and shifted gears.

Gingerly, he turned the ignition key to start the motor. Pressing his feet hard on the brake and clutch, he jiggled the gear shift into what he hoped was the first position. He held his breath, moved his foot off the brake to the accelerator, and released the clutch. With the sound of grating metal and screeching rubber, the Jeep lurched forward. Gene drove in first gear for several seconds. He dreaded to shift again. With almost a mile to drive and Skipper gasping for breath, he shoved the clutch to the floor, jostled the gearshift up to the right, and the same horror repeated itself. A passing G.I. put his fingers into his ears.

Gene decided to drive the rest of the way at thirty miles per hour in second gear. He heard the motor groaning and hoped the transmission would survive the abuse.

With a sigh of relief, he pulled into the parking area in front of the entrance to the infirmary. Skipper's breathing was irregular, and he appeared barely conscious.

Gene, in his excitement, took his foot off the accelerator and stepped hard on the brake. The Jeep jolted and stalled, pitching him into the steering wheel and dumping Skipper onto the floor. "I didn't shift into neutral!"

"For God's sake, Lieutenant, where the hell did you learn how to drive?" shouted a major glaring at Gene.

"I never learned how to drive, sir," he responded, lifting Skipper into his arms and rushing toward the infirmary.

The major shook his head in astonishment. "It's not to be believed! He flies a four-engine bomber and doesn't know how to drive a car!"

Gene hurried past him holding Skipper, who resembled a milk-chocolate replica from a Fanny Farmer Sweet Shoppe.

The infirmary, a temporary structure, much the same as all the other buildings at Great Ashfield, was thrown together to accommodate the influx of combat crews from the United States. Its interior was austere, and Gene was immediately engulfed in medicinal and antiseptic odors. He ran to the admissions desk, cradling his trembling pet in his arms.

"My dog's in trouble, Corporal. I'm hoping someone here can do something to help him. He almost drowned in a drainage ditch, and I'm afraid he might die!"

"Come with me, Lieutenant. Maybe the emergency team

can do something to help him." They rushed through a pair of swinging doors and entered a large room sectioned off with cloth screens. Busy medics were attending two airmen wounded in yesterday's mission. He could see that one had a bandaged head and the other was receiving a blood transfusion.

"Doctor, I'm sorry to bring a dog in here," said the corporal. "But he's all choked up with muddy water and he looks like he's half dead!"

Captain Huff, the group Flight Surgeon, turned toward Gene and Skipper. "I don't know if there's anything we can do, Lieutenant. This isn't an animal hospital!"

"Oh, the poor dog!" cried a nurse. She rushed past Doc Huff and snatched Skipper from Gene's arms.

"Jackson," said the doctor, with a look of resignation, "get some paper and a couple of towels spread out on that table, and we're going to need oxygen and suction."

The lanky medical tech flew into action, and the nurse placed Skipper on the table, holding him firmly with both hands.

"Lieutenant, we're going to do the best we can for your dog," the doc said. "Please wait outside in the anteroom, and we'll come out to brief you as soon as we're finished."

Gene left and sat down on a bench near the corporal's desk. "Thanks a lot for your help."

"Forget it, Lieutenant. Let's hope he'll be O.K.," he answered and continued typing.

After several minutes, Gene looked at his watch. Impatiently, he paced the floor. *What will I say to the guys if he doesn't make it? They'll never forgive me. After all we've been through taking care of him, he drowns in a drainage ditch.* His thoughts grew morbid, and he imagined a scenario of being shot down over Germany because of losing their good luck charm. *Poor Skipper! It's all my fault that this happened to you.*

"Would you mind sitting down, Lieutenant? Your pacing is distracting me."

"I'm sorry, Corporal." Gene sat down, nervously drumming his fingers on his knees. The second hand on the wall clock behind the desk jumped audibly, marking its progress, which felt painfully slow. *They've been at it for twenty minutes already,* he thought. "What the hell's going on in there?" he asked aloud.

The swinging doors opened, and the nurse who came to Skipper's aid entered the anteroom.

Gene jumped to his feet.

"We've got your dog stabilized, Lieutenant. We think that we flushed out all the mud and water, but it's too soon to tell if he'll have a complete recovery. We gave him a mild tranquilizer, and he's resting quietly. It's best that you wait here for a while longer. You can help yourself to some coffee over on that table." She cast her eyes at his mud-covered pants and encrusted shoes. "You've really been through an awful time, haven't you?" Gene noticed her soft, wide-set eyes and sympathetic smile. "I know how you feel. I had to leave my golden retriever Jake with my parents when I enlisted in the service."

"You don't know the half of it. I had to borrow a Jeep about a mile from here, and you may not believe this, but

I never learned how to drive. I hope I didn't screw up the transmission."

The nurse burst out laughing. "I'm not making fun of you, Lieutenant. It's just so preposterous seeing a pair of silver wings on a guy who doesn't know how to drive. Where are you from?"

"I grew up on the sidewalks of New York City in a neighborhood where the only ones who drove cars were Good Humor men and garbage collectors. Now I need someone to take me back to Squadron Headquarters. The sergeant who loaned me the Jeep must be wondering where I am."

"No problem, Lieutenant. I'll drive you." She turned to the corporal. "Please tell everyone inside that I'll be back in a few minutes." A smile was still plastered on her face.

A suspicious noise accompanied the gear-shifting, but the ride back to Headquarters was pleasant. Gene found it easy to talk to this outgoing nurse, and he thought how nice it would be to get to know her better.

The sergeant was waiting in the parking area. When he spied his Jeep, he raised his hands with a puzzled look on his face. "What's with the chauffeur, Lieutenant?"

"Never mind. It's a long story. Would you please give us a ride back to the infirmary?"

The nurse looked down at her feet. Still giggling, she climbed into the rear seat, and the bewildered sergeant hopped in behind the wheel.

Gene tensed up hearing the noise of metal against metal when the gears shifted. The sergeant shook his head but made no comment.

"Thanks a million. It meant a lot to me," said Gene as the Jeep came to a stop in front of the building.

"I hope your little dog will be O.K. And, Lieutenant, I have a pretty good idea what the long story's about!" He drove off with the gears clanking.

"I'll pop into the Emergency Room to see what's happening with your dog, and I'll be right out to give you an update," said the nurse.

Gene stood breathing heavily, finding it difficult to swallow. *What if he's alive but disabled?* he thought. *What if we have to make a decision to put him to sleep?* He felt nauseous and sat down on the bench, head thrown back, eyes closed.

The sound of a swinging door brought Gene to his feet. "Look who we have here, Lieutenant," said the nurse, carrying a wriggling puppy in her arms. "He's all yours, and he'll be just fine. Try to keep him quiet for the rest of the day." She planted a kiss on Skipper's muddy head and asked, "What's his name?"

"Skipper, and I'm Gene. We've been through this ordeal together, and I don't even know what to call you," he said to the nurse.

"Just call me Softie." She smiled. "Hi, Skipper. Please come and visit us when you're all cleaned up. You can ask for Ginny Garwood." She handed Skipper to Gene and asked, "Would you like me to give you both a ride back to your barracks?"

"That would be great!" he replied.

They climbed into her Jeep with a large Red Cross on the hood, Gene holding Skipper firmly on his lap. Crumbs of dried mud fell to the floor as he stroked his lovable pet. Skipper responded with a couple of licks on Gene's nose and chin. All felt right with the world.

"I can't thank you enough, Ginny, for all you've done," said Gene as they approached the squadron compound. "It was above and beyond the call of duty. I'd like to take you to supper tomorrow night. There's a charming little pub in Stowmarket that can put together a few tasty dishes despite rationing. Of course, I'm assuming we'll make it back from our mission."

Ginny's eyes softened, and her smile changed as she seemed to take in the full reality of his invitation. "I'd love to! See you at seven—and I'll do the driving!"

Gene carried Skipper toward the barracks, secretly hoping to have some time to change his clothes and to brush some of the caked mud off Skipper's coat. Instead, he was greeted by looks of bewilderment and a chorus of questions.

"What the hell happened to the two of you?" cried J.O.

"Where did you take him?" asked Al.

"What a mess! How are we gonna get him cleaned up?" questioned Bob.

Gene recounted Skipper's misadventure and the wonderful treatment he received at the infirmary. He was careful to omit the debacle of his first driving experience.

"We're lucky that they were able to revive him!" said Al. "I'll bathe him in the latrine. The sink should be large enough."

"I'll go with you," said Gene, grabbing a few towels.

The latrine was divided into three sections, and each held

a half-dozen toilets, community showers, and washbasins. Captain Art Johnson was shaving near the far end. At first, he ignored Skipper's presence. Then Al ran the water full force and dunked an unsuspecting Skipper into the warm bath. A startling yelp, with violent splashing, brought an angry outburst from the foam-faced captain. "For God's sake, Lages, don't bathe that filthy mutt in a sink that we wash our hands and faces in!"

Although annoyed, Gene decided that it wasn't worth the confrontation, especially since their efforts were turning into a fiasco. The sink wasn't deep enough anyway. "Why don't we fill this garbage can with water and drag it outside?" he suggested.

"Half full," Al countered. "Maybe less than half full. One drowning a day is enough."

The captain turned toward them, drying his face. He stared at the shaking dog, his eyes taking in Gene's grimy shoes and filthy pants. With a contrite grin, he said, "Let me help, fellas."

CHAPTER FIVE
Skipper Shares a Loss

On the morning of May twelfth, all sixteen officers in the barracks, along with the rest of the 385th, reported for briefing. This mission was to be a maximum effort, with almost one thousand Fortresses and Liberators taking part in a two-pronged attack on the oil refineries at Leipzig and the fighter plane factories at Zwickau.

Gene scanned the clouds floating in the sky like enormous tufts of cotton. The morning air was damp and smelled of wet grass. He climbed aboard the truck for the ride to the flight line along with J.O., Bob, Al, and John Demereaux's crew.

"This is our sixteenth, John," Gene said. "Only nine more to go."

"Seven for us," he replied. "That's a good number."

The rest of J.O.'s crew was already at the hardstand when the truck arrived.

The four officers jumped off and Gene waved to John. "See ya up there in a little while. We're flying together in the same three-ship element."

Assembling the huge armada over England was lengthy and complicated. The parade of planes that finally headed for the English Channel was divided into fifty-four ship combat wings separated at three-minute intervals. The result resembled enormous formations of migrating geese.

Approximately halfway across Germany, the combat wings assigned to hit Zwickau turned and headed southeastward toward their target, located forty miles north of the Czechoslovakian border.

Gene monitored the inter-plane channel to listen for orders from the group commander in the lead plane, whose call sign was "Hot-Shot-Yellow." J.O. had his headset tuned to the plane's intercom.

Looking through his overhead window, Gene was startled to see many contrails streaming a few thousand feet above their formation. He switched his radio to the intercom position and reported, "Co-pilot to crew. There's a helluva lot of contrails high above us. I can't make out who they are. Keep your head and eyes moving. Over." He turned back to the group channel.

Shortly after, a message came loud and clear. "Hot-Shot-Yellow to group. Enemy fighters eleven o'clock high. Watch them. Over."

Gene immediately switched back to intercom. "Copilot to crew. Hot-Shot-Yellow reports enemy fighters in the area."

"Pilot to crew. There are three large fighter groups above and in front of us. Have your guns ready for an attack."

"Pilot to Navigator. Bob, you better make note of where we are."

"Pilot to Co-pilot. I'm gonna get on the group channel, Gene. You stay on the intercom."

The first formation of fighters turned downward and headed directly toward the Fortresses, their guns blazing.

"Co-pilot to crew. Here they come!"

The plane trembled as their .50-caliber machine guns poured a stream of lead at the attacking Messerschmitt 109s.

Chaos ensued. Bombers and fighters exploded and went down in flames all over the sky. Parachutes descended as crewmen abandoned burning planes twisting out of control.

No sooner had the first wave of fighters dived beneath the Fortresses, than a second wave began their onslaught.

J.O. and Gene remained silent while each crewmember shouted out the positions of the attacking enemy planes.

POW! The window above Gene's head was blown out, and the deafening concussion from Charlie Bond's twin .50-caliber guns, only inches away, caused a throbbing pain in his ears.

It wasn't over yet. Another group pivoted and came plummeting down at the battered Fortresses. It was almost impossible to keep track of the losses.

Out of his right window, Gene was blinded by the white and garish orange flashes of an exploding Fortress. It was John Demereaux and his crewmates. There couldn't be any survivors. He was horrified.

The enemy fighters departed for their home base, leaving the mauled bombers to regroup and continue their mission to Zwickau.

"Hot-Shot-Yellow to group. Let's fill in the gaps and tighten up this formation. We don't want any stragglers to be picked off."

At Zwickau, the antiaircraft barrages seemed insignificant compared to the nightmarish attack by the German fighters. The factories were well targeted and pulverized.

Their mission accomplished, the bombers turned westward, heading home.

"Pilot to crew. Thank God that's over. We'll sure remember this one!"

"Bombardier to crew. Let's have a status report on your guns and ammunition."

Gene was alarmed to hear that five gun positions were burned out or ammunition-spent.

About halfway across Germany, he began to relax, but not for long. Seemingly, from out of nowhere, a swarm of more than fifty Focke-Wulf 190 German fighters bore down on the crippled groups of Fortresses. Like a scene from a Hollywood movie, German planes whipsawed through the formations in groups of three and four from every direction.

The crew did their best with the guns that were still operative. It was a repeat performance of what had occurred earlier in the mission.

"Co-pilot to crew. Be sure you have your chutes hooked to your harnesses. We may have to leave this plane in a helluva hurry!"

It was beginning to appear hopeless.

"Hot-Shot-Yellow to group. Be ready to fire green/green flares on my command."

Gene hoped that they would be seen by Allied fighters somewhere in the vicinity. Green/green flares were standard procedure for bombers under enemy attack.

"Co-pilot to Engineer. Charlie, get ready to fire your green/green flares on my signal. Over."

"Engineer to Copilot. Roger. I'm ready when you are."

Then came the signal from the group commander, and all planes released their flares, filling the sky with a display of eerie fireworks. This procedure was repeated four times during the ongoing battle.

"Hot-Shot-Yellow to group. There are two large formations of fighters approaching from three o'clock."

Gene's muscles tightened at the sight of the approaching planes. He knew that there would be little chance of surviving another attack. He reached beneath his seat to be sure his chest chute was available. He knew it could be a matter of minutes before he and the crew might have to bail out.

All at once a voice screamed across the radio. "They're P-38s!"

Cheers went through the airwaves as if a heaven-sent host of angels had come to their rescue.

"Hello, Big Brothers. Hello, Big Brothers. This is Little Friends. Over."

"Hot-Shot-Yellow to Little Friends. Are we ever glad to see you guys. Over."

"Little Friends to Hot-Shot-Yellow. Tell your gunners to

cease firing. Tell your gunners to cease firing. We'll take care of this."

Gene watched with exhilaration as the P-38s battled the German fighters, destroying many and driving off the rest.

The remaining Fortresses returned to their base at Great Ashfield, shepherded by their P-38 escorts. The losses for the day were forty-five bombers, ten American fighters, and over one hundred German planes.

Everyone in the truck was silent on the ride back to the barracks. Gene had difficulty organizing his thoughts and emotions, experiencing an all-pervasive sadness. The empty cots of his four bunkmates who would not be returning magnified the loss he felt.

In no mood to reciprocate Skipper's joyous welcome, he sat down on his cot and stared out the window. Rejected by Gene, Skipper pranced back and forth, bringing various toys to J.O., Al, and Bob, but none of them would play.

"Woof, woof," he yapped, with his head on his paws, rump raised. "Woof, woof," he continued. "Woof, woof!"

"Why the hell don't you do what that mutt is asking for?" shouted Lieutenant Stahlburg from across the room.

"I'll discuss it with him," retorted Gene.

Doc Huff arrived, his expression projecting a deep feeling of sympathy for what the men in his charge had been through. He handed everyone a sleeping pill. "This'll help you get a good night's rest. You won't be flying in the morning." He patted Skipper's head before leaving and with a smile said, "Glad you're all better, little fella. These guys really need you."

Skipper reached up and put his paw on Gene's arm and let out a muffled whimper. The wrinkles above his golden brows gave him an expression of worry, while his large, pleading eyes stared with intensity. "C'mon, Skipper, let's go for a walk. We can both use some fresh air."

Spying the leash, he danced in circles, hardly remaining still long enough for Gene to hook him up.

Once outside, Skipper raised his head, sniffing the air as if he could taste it. The late spring afternoon was sunny and filled with the earthy aromas of the lovely English countryside.

Walking along the road bordering plowed fields, Gene noted the rows of baby Brussels sprouts peeking their green heads above the furrows. The atmosphere of serenity seemed incongruous compared to the violence that had occurred only a few hours earlier.

They continued along the road, circling back toward the squadron administrative buildings. The sky was streaked with billowy orange and pink clouds, colored by the late afternoon sun. Skipper continued to explore as if he might uncover a hidden treasure.

Gene had stopped to admire nature's artistry when he caught sight of the American flag, rippling in the gentle breeze. There it was, a piece of home, a symbol of belonging, the reason for being where he was.

He thought about his dinner date with Ginny. No way could he be good company this evening. He walked into the Charge of Quarters' office and made the call. Ginny answered.

"Hi, this is Gene."

"Thank heaven you made it back! We're all so heartbroken at the losses today."

"It was rough. Some of our bunkmates were shot down. Could we postpone our date for a few days?"

"I'm so sorry, but my transfer came through as a flight nurse with the 27th Air Transport group, and I'm leaving Great Ashfield in the morning."

"Let's stay in touch. Send me your address as soon as you know it. I'm sure we'll find a way to get together. You'll make a great flight nurse!"

"I'm looking forward to it. Please take care of yourself!"

When Gene and Skipper returned, Captain Ed Stern was doing a chore that was hard to watch. It was his responsibility to collect each of the missing officer's personal effects to be sent home to their families.

He had already started to lay out various items on John Demereaux's cot when Gene noticed the eight-by-ten picture of John's wife and infant son, which he had frequently admired. There it was, along with stacks of letters, snapshots, and various pieces of military jewelry. The only items of clothing included were his Class A dress uniform and hat. It was painful to imagine the grief that would accompany the arrival of this package.

Skipper, watching the activity on John's cot, where he was always welcome, hopped up among the items Ed Stern had carefully assembled. Taken aback, Gene gave Skipper a stinging rap on his behind with the back of his hand. Skipper gave a frightened yelp and leaped to the floor. With his head bent, he hurried to the far end of the room and crawled under one of the beds. He had never been spanked before.

Ed Stern gathered the last of the items into a carton, and before he left, he turned to Gene and the other three officers and said, "Why don't you guys get out of here for awhile? Have some supper and a good stiff drink at the Officers Club."

The atmosphere of the mess hall was solemn, and Gene felt no solace in being among the men. He had little appetite and felt ashamed of himself for having lost his temper. In a hurry to return to Skipper, he gathered extra food in his mess kit, declined the drink at the Officers Club, and went back to apologize to his little pal. "Here, Skipper. Look at the nice supper I brought you."

Skipper poked his head from under the bed, where he had taken refuge, cautiously walked over to Gene's cot, and sat at his feet.

Gene reached down and gathered the dog into his arms. With hugs and kisses, he said, "I'm sorry I spanked you. I love you very much, and I hope you're still my friend." Skipper responded with his own display of affection, washing Gene's face with his tongue from ear to ear. He didn't know how to be angry. There was no drink in the Officers Club that could have been as satisfying a tonic.

With Skipper pressed alongside him that night, Gene quietly cried himself to sleep.

CHAPTER SIX

Skipper's Longest Day

J.O. managed to arrange a much needed three-day leave for his crew. They were lucky to have Gat available to take care of Skipper.

The top priority for their first afternoon in London was a pub in Knightsbridge run by a middle-aged, heavy-set lady with a Cockney accent. She was jovial, gossipy, and warm-hearted. Strawberry blond curls, illuminated by the overhead fixtures, spotlighted her as if she were the star of an unnamed play.

She adored the American airmen and reveled in the fact that her pub was adopted as a hangout for the guys of the Mighty Eighth. The walls were covered from ceiling to floor with photographs of bomber crews and fighter pilots. Gene took pride in the fact that his crew's photograph was represented. The exchange of stories with former classmates from flying schools back in the States was cathartic.

Later in the afternoon, they took a cab to the fashionable Grosvenor House across from Hyde Park, revamped to accommodate a spacious Officers Club. Gene was hungry and knew that there would be an assortment of snacks to nibble on. Food rationing resulted in sparse restaurant menus, to say the least.

There was much camaraderie and sharing of experiences, and Gene's spirits lifted. Scanning the faces of J.O., Bob, and Al, he could see the return of their cheerfulness as well.

Early the next morning, in his room at the Strand Palace Hotel, Gene was abruptly awakened by a knock on the door. Before he could respond, a silver-haired grandmotherly figure bearing a butler's tray burst into the room with a cheery admonishment. "I 'ope you're not going to spend this lovely spring mornin' in bed." She pushed Gene forward, stuffed two pillows behind his back, and arranged the tray across his lap. "Ow about some nice 'ot porridge, a biscuit, jam, and coffee to start your day off?"

Gene was delighted and felt special with this unexpected amenity, standard at the Strand Palace, the war notwithstanding.

Cradled in the comfort of an especially thick mattress, supported by feathery pillows, and enjoying his sweetened porridge, he smiled, knowing this same wake-up scenario was happening with Bob, Al, and J.O.

With only nine more missions to go, he felt optimistic and hoped that the worst of it was behind them. Not wanting to waste time, he finished his breakfast, grabbed an oversized towel, and hurried down the hall to one of the shared bathrooms.

He entered an immaculately maintained white-tiled room, decorated with blue and white striped wallpaper and dominated by a large bathtub, no shower. On the wall facing him was a large sign in bold letters:

"REMEMBER THE SIX INCH BATH."

Gene chuckled, accommodating the request.

A cheerful foursome met in the hotel lobby, grinning from their obviously shared royal treatment.

That afternoon, they went to two different movie theaters to see "Up in Arms" with Danny Kaye, and "Going My Way" with Bing Crosby. The muffled sound of air raid sirens and the dull thud of distant antiaircraft guns during one of Bing's songs preceded the warning flashed along the bottom of the screen: "We are under attack by enemy bombers. Patrons may leave for air raid shelters. The movie will continue." Gene found it amusing that no one left.

On their last day in London, they decided to visit its famous sights. Gene felt refreshed and relaxed although apprehensive about returning to Great Ashfield and aerial combat. They hailed several cabs before finding a driver who accepted their bid of a flat fee to act as their tour guide. The first stop was Buckingham Palace, followed by Westminster Abbey and St. Paul's Cathedral. They continued past the Houses of Parliament, Ten Downing Street, and the Tower of London. "It's a miracle that all of these places are still standing," observed J.O.

Their guide insisted on showing them neighborhoods with skeletal shells of bombed-out buildings and streets piled with rubble. "I hope you Yanks are paying them back for all this," he said.

It was one o'clock in the afternoon when the group arrived at Euston Station for their trip back to East Anglia. The timetables were unreliable since priority was given to trains transporting military hardware and troops. It was impossible to determine a time of arrival. At four, they finally arrived at Stowmarket, the nearest train depot to Great Ashfield.

When they at last made it back to their barracks, they found Gat alone with Skipper, who was beside himself with joy at their return.

"Have I got something to show youse guys!" said Gat with a broad smile. "Have a seat, fellas, and I'll present our new star." Everyone sat down on the nearest cot.

"This oughta be good," said J.O.

"C'mere, Skippa," called Gat, holding a piece of KRation biscuit in his hand. "Let's have a song and dance." Skipper stood on his hind legs, front paws gracefully dangling, balancing his body in a ballet posture, hopping in circles, yipping and barking his song. Gene and the others exploded in delighted laughter and applause as Gat rewarded Skipper for his performance.

"How long did it take you to teach him to do that?" asked J.O.

"I been woikin' on it for about a month," answered Gat

proudly. "Me and Skippa get along great. But he knows who's the boss," he added with a sheepish grin.

"What's been going on, Gat, while we were on leave?" asked Gene.

There was a momentary silence, which made him feel uneasy.

"Well, the 385th lost three crews, but none in our squadron…and, and…" He hesitated. "There's a notice hung in the latrine youse guys should see."

"I'll go take a look," Gene volunteered. He hurried to the bulletin board where information and important directives were frequently posted.

Instead of the familiar Alert or Stand-down signs, Gene was jolted by an order from Eighth Air Force headquarters, signed by General James Doolittle:

Effective this date, the tour of combat for all Eighth Air Force Bomber Crews is increased from twenty-five to thirty missions. These orders affect all crews who have not yet flown their twenty-fifth mission.

Gene swallowed hard. It felt as though he had just read a death sentence. Instead of having only nine missions left to fly, they would now have fourteen.

He rushed back to his crewmates. "You're not going to believe what's on that bulletin board!" He repeated the order from General Doolittle.

J.O., Bob, and Al looked at Gene in shocked disbelief.

"We went off to London thinking we were on the home

stretch with just nine more to fly," said Bob, "and now we're only at the halfway mark."

"How about those poor bastards that completed twenty-four missions and thought they had one more to go?" asked Al.

With his eyes downcast, J.O. bitterly pronounced, "All I can say is twenty-five for God and Country and five for Jimmy Doolittle."

During the last two weeks in May, both the RAF and American Air Forces flew maximum-effort missions all day and night, pounding German air bases and transportation hubs.

On June fifth, Gene was amazed that they were called for a briefing at five o'clock in the afternoon. The mission was to bomb the railroad marshaling yards, a sprawling complex at Versailles, outside of Paris.

"I wonder what jackass at Eighth Air Force headquarters came up with the stupid idea to blow up a bunch of railroad tracks at this hour of the evening," said Gene. "They'll have them fixed and working again in just a couple of days."

"They must have run out of ideas for better targets," said J.O. with a look of disdain.

Takeoff time was six P.M. Antiaircraft fire at Versailles was moderate, and the mission was completed with only minor damage and no loss of planes.

At ten P.M., after debriefing and supper, they hurried back to Skipper. As soon as he saw his friends, he nudged his empty dish and performed the now standard song and dance routine. The song sounded more plaintive and scolding because the little dog's canine clock had been disrupted. He had never eaten supper this late before.

"All right, Skipper, you can stop complaining," said Gene, emptying the mess kit into the bowl. "Here's some nice Spam, potato hash, and Brussels sprouts. I hope you enjoy it more than we did."

Skipper wolfed down the meal, then selected one of his squeaky toys, dropping it into J.O.'s lap.

"This is the last thing I feel like doing right now," said J.O., tossing the rubber toy across the floor.

"O.K.," said Gene, "I'll take him for a quick walk."

The air felt wet and a fog enfolded them. The blackout conditions, added to the eeriness of the setting, reminded Gene of a scene from Sir Arthur Conan Doyle's Sherlock Holmes novel, *The Hound of the Baskervilles*.

He also wondered about the Alert sign posted in the latrine, indicating a mission scheduled for the morning. *Wouldn't it be nice if they scrubbed it,* he thought.

"What a soggy mess out there," said Gene on his return. Skipper shook from head to tail, ridding himself of the dampness that had penetrated his furry coat.

J.O. patted Skipper's clammy head. "I doubt that we'll be able to fly in the morning if it doesn't clear up out there."

"Well, let's turn in now and get some shut-eye," said Bob. "Gat'll be in for the wake-up around four or five, which gives us only a few hours to sleep."

Everyone agreed.

Gene stretched out under the covers. Skipper hopped up to join him, aligning himself with Gene's spine. It was impossible to move with Skipper's body locking the blanket in place. The faint odor of damp fur added to the discomfort, as did Skipper's rhythmic snoring.

It seemed that only minutes had passed when the door was flung open and Gat marched in, turning on the lights.

"Da followin' officers will report for briefin' at 0200." Before he could announce any names, there was a raucous uproar from everyone, with several shoes flying through the air at the unwelcome charge of quarters.

"For God's sake, Gat, it's only twelve thirty, and we just turned out the lights a little while ago," yelled one of the annoyed officers. "You must have your signals mixed."

"Who in the hell is scheduling a briefing at two in the morning?" asked Gene.

"I can't help it. I asked da same question when da briefin' officer at group headquarters gave me deese instructions."

"This routine is getting nuttier by the hour," said Al. "First they send us on a stupid mission to blow up a bunch of railroad tracks, and now they call us to a briefing in the middle of the night."

"Someone's trying to make a grandstand play at our expense," grumbled Norman Robbins, pilot of one of the replacement crews.

"Maybe they're sending us to Burma to bomb the Japs," said Bob.

Skipper ran from one man to the other, barking as if to ask, "What's going on here?"

Looks of disgust were stamped on many faces as the truck headed for the mess hall. Bob was scowling, Al's jaw was clenched, and J.O. kept rubbing the sleep out of his eyes.

"Who feels like eating anything? We just had supper two and a half hours ago," said Gene. "We might as well stay on the truck and go straight up to the Ready Room."

Crowds of officers had gathered in the lobby before they arrived. The enlisted men were already inside being briefed, which allowed them time to prepare the planes for the mission, loading machine gun ammo, checking instruments, and warming up engines.

"Look at all the MPs! I wonder what they're doing here," said Al.

"Who the hell knows?" answered J.O. "This whole thing seems weird."

An explosion of applause and whistling came from inside the Ready Room.

Gene stared at the other officers, searching their faces for some clue of what might be going on "What are those guys cheering at?" he asked in amazement.

"Damned if I know," said Al.

"Hey, I'll bet Bob Hope is in there entertaining, and that's why they woke us up so early," said J.O.

As soon as the enlisted men left the rear exit of the Ready Room, the officers filed in and took their seats. "This oughta be good," said Gene in anticipation.

Colonel Elliott Vandevanter, a much respected and revered West Point officer, stood tall on the platform. "Good morning, gentlemen. I've got some exciting news for you." He paused for a few seconds. "This is it! Today is D-Day!"

It was electrifying. The whole group jumped to their feet, welcoming the announcement they thought would never come. Two staff officers dramatically flung back a curtain, revealing a room-sized map of the five Normandy invasion beaches.

"Let's quiet down, fellas," ordered Colonel Van. "Before we get into the details of the mission, I have some messages I want to read to you. The first is from our Supreme Commanding Officer, General Eisenhower:

'Soldiers, sailors, and airmen of the Allied Expeditionary Forces: You are about to embark upon the great crusade toward which we have striven these many months. The eyes of the world are upon you. The hopes and prayers of liberty-loving people everywhere march with you. The tide has turned. I have full confidence in your courage, devotion to duty, and skill in battle. We will accept nothing less than full victory.'"

This was followed by equally stirring prayers from President Franklin Roosevelt and Prime Minister Winston Churchill.

Gene choked up with the words that summed up his own feelings: "a struggle to preserve the republic, the religion, the civilization, and to set free a suffering humanity." Every nerve in his body was on edge with excitement.

This was the day that they all had waited for. It would no longer be a lonely and seemingly futile war, fought by the American and Royal Air Forces. They would now be joined by the Allied armies.

"Let's get to the details," said Colonel Van after a respectful pause. "There will be three missions flown today. Our group and many others will be flying the first and third. The initial target will be Omaha Beach, and we will be dropping our bombs twenty minutes before our troops come ashore.

"The weather is lousy, and there will be a radar plane leading each combat wing. Warships and landing craft of the Allied Invasion Fleet will be fifteen hundred yards offshore. Therefore, woe be the bombardier who drops his bombs short this morning.

"We'll be flying for the first time with Royal Air Force fighters and bombers. There will be no, I repeat, *no* test firing of guns. We can't afford any mistaken aircraft recognition. All guns will be loaded and parked. We don't think you have to be worried about enemy planes because you'll be escorted by more than three thousand Allied fighters.

"We are starting so early this morning because of the length of time necessary to organize the thousands of planes participating in this mission. Are there any questions?"

There were none.

"Okay! Get out to your planes, give 'em hell, and good luck!"

On the ride to their hardstand, Gene felt uneasy with the enveloping fog reducing visibility to a mere few hundred feet. The excitement, however, minimized his concern. He would be participating in the most spectacular military event in history: three thousand fighters, not to mention thousands of bombers, in the air at the same time. "It'll be a miracle if all of us climb through this soup without midair collisions," said Gene.

"We'll just have to trust fate," answered J.O. "What else can we do?"

Because there was little forward visibility, Gene and J.O. handled the controls together on the takeoff. J.O. on the wheel and Gene on the rudder pedals kept the plane parallel to the side of the runway. Charlie Bond stood between the two pilots' seats, reading air speed from the indicator for J.O., and they lifted the plane safely off the ground.

Every few minutes, Gene was startled by a shadowy whoosh streaking in front of their windshield. At approximately nineteen thousand feet, they climbed into the clear above the clouds to witness a remarkable sight. Planes were poking up into the sky by the hundreds, resembling an overflowing popcorn machine in a movie theater.

Gene and J.O. looked for their group leader, who would be intermittently firing red/green flares.

All of the other group leaders would also be firing flares of different color combinations to pull their planes together. Flying in circles, J.O. and Gene finally spotted the lead Fortress and took their assigned position with the 385th.

Those who couldn't find their group tagged on to the nearest formation as was anticipated during the various briefings. It created an appearance of organized chaos.

Colonel Van, in charge of leading the 385th, would now have to move his group to join the 447th and the 94th. Together, they made up the fifty-four planes of the Fourth Combat Wing.

They took their position in the Eighth Air Force assemblage over Bury St. Edmunds. What at first appeared to be aerial gridlock and confusion settled into a majestic panorama of planes spanning the skies over England in every direction as far as the eye could see.

Heady with a sense of purpose, pride, and righteousness, Gene knew that this was the beginning of the end of the war.

A squadron of Royal Air Force Spitfires flew by, waggling their wings in greeting to the American bombers. It brought to mind Winston Churchill's memorable tribute to those courageous, outnumbered British fighter pilots who defeated Hermann Goering's Luftwaffe during the Battle of Britain. "Never in the field of human conflict was so much owed by so many to so few."

Approaching the English coast, Colonel Van radioed: "Hot-Shot-Yellow to group. Bomb bay doors open."

How extraordinary it seemed to Gene for a bomb run to start at the English Channel.

Minutes later, the group made their drop over Omaha Beach and turned back for the flight to Great Ashfield. They encountered neither antiaircraft fire nor enemy fighters.

Gene tuned the plane's radio to the British Broadcasting Company: "Berlin Radio reports that the Normandy coast is under intense bombardment by planes of the Allied Air Forces." He smiled with satisfaction as they headed home.

After debriefing, all crews were ordered to remain in the Ready Room to await their next assignment.

Gene felt a feverish level of excess energy. He was anxious to learn what was happening on the beaches. Everyone else was asking the same question. "What's going on?" He looked at his watch. It was only ten A.M. and already they had been waiting more than an hour to hear about their next mission. Nothing was happening. Gene was becoming impatient.

He walked out to the lobby, where a coffee urn and paper cups were set up on a metal folding table. Much to his surprise, he saw Gat standing among the group drinking coffee.

"Hey, Gat, what are you doing up here on the flight line?"

"Captain Stern ordered all Squadron administrative people out heah to help load gas and bombs for da next mission."

Gene walked back inside with his coffee cup. "Would you believe I just ran into Gat out there in the lobby?" he said to Al.

"Yeah? What's he doing up here?"

"All the Squadron office staff were ordered up to the flight line to help load bombs and gas."

Al shook his head. "What does Gat know about servicing planes?"

Gene shrugged.

By two o'clock in the afternoon, there was still no activity or information concerning the next mission. Gene thought of Skipper locked up in the barracks. "J.O., did you happen to notice if there was any water in Skipper's bowl before we left?"

"It wouldn't have occurred to me," answered J.O. "Gat looks after it."

"But Gat's been up here all day long. I think I'll hitch a ride back, give Skipper some water and take him for a quick walk."

But when Gene got to the road, he found it blocked by a military police Jeep.

"Sorry, Lieutenant, no one is permitted to leave the flight line until after all missions are completed," said an M.P.

Thwarted, Gene marched back inside.

"The MPs won't let anyone leave the area," reported Gene. "Poor dog. It'll be nighttime before we get back from wherever the hell they send us." He could imagine Skipper, confused and agitated, alone in the dark barracks.

"Some mess we'll walk into when we get back tonight," said Al. "He'll probably piss on somebody's bed, to say the least of what we'll be tramping into."

"He must be thirsty as hell in that hot barracks with the windows shut. The poor dog!" Gene repeated.

J.O. tilted his head toward the ceiling, and with outstretched arms, intoned, "Life will go on, Gene. Life will go on."

"I can't believe we're having this stupid conversation," said Bob. "We just took part in the invasion of Normandy. God knows what those guys are going through on the beaches, and here we are worrying about Skipper peeing on someone's bed."

Gene felt embarrassed.

At three P.M., when they were called to attention, they were hungry, tired, bored, and anxious. "Quiet down, everybody," said the briefing officer. "The German High Command has moved strong reinforcements of tanks and artillery into and around Caen. The British and Canadian troops who came ashore at Sword and Juno beaches are being hammered by them. They haven't been able to consolidate their positions."

He pointed to the large map showing the location of the enemy armor. "We'll be going in low and you can expect some pretty serious antiaircraft fire. All crewmembers should be cautioned to wear their flak vests and helmets. Unfortunately, the target area includes some of the built-up sections of the town, so keep your formation as tight as possible. It will help minimize the civilian damage. The mission will include a total of three hundred Fortresses."

The weather had cleared since the morning mission. By six-thirty P.M., they were crossing the Channel and approaching the coast of Normandy. The spectacle of scattered debris in the water and along the edges of the beach told a grim story.

"Heaven help them," Gene prayed silently. A sickening thought crossed his mind. *What if they don't make it?*

Nearing Caen, they were met by accurate antiaircraft fire and at only twelve thousand feet were easy targets for the German gunners.

"Ball Turret to crew. It looks like we've leveled half the town. I hope to hell all those people are in shelters. We'll probably never know how many we killed or wounded."

On the return trip to Great Ashfield, Gene had mixed emotions of relief and sorrow. There was also an awareness of his participation in a day of momentous history.

At the debriefing, Colonel Vandevanter announced that all landings were successful and the beachheads secured. There were rounds of cheers and applause.

By the time they got to the mess hall, Gene was exhausted and famished. The crew had had neither food nor sleep in the past twenty-two hours.

Tables were covered with small paper cups of whiskey to celebrate the day's event. Gene grabbed one and gulped it down. With his stomach empty, the alcohol moved rapidly to his head and he staggered to the chow line. Barely sober enough to accumulate extra helpings for Skipper, Gene scarfed down his supper and raced back to the barracks. The others followed.

They found Static draped across the entryway. Skipper gave a scratchy, hoarse yelp on the other side of the door. Hurrying inside, followed by Static, they were greeted by a frenzied, wild-eyed pet.

Al snatched Skipper's empty bowl and went outside to fill it with water. Bob ran from cot to cot, feeling for wet spots on the blankets, while J.O. and Gene mopped up the puddles on the floor with sections of the Stars and Stripes newspaper.

"Who would've imagined this as a finale to D-Day?" said J.O., gingerly holding the soggy bouquet of peesoaked newspaper between his thumb and forefinger.

"We better pack it in," said Al, returning with the filled bowl. "They have the Alert sign in the latrine. We're flying another one tomorrow." He placed the dish in front of his little friend.

Skipper slurped greedily and allowed Static to share his drink with him. All four grinned at the picture of the black and tan pooches rhythmically guzzling the water. Their enjoyment reminded Gene of his favorite egg cream special at the corner soda fountain.

"We damned well better get some sleep tonight," said J.O.

"C'mon, Static. Let's get you home," said Bob, slipping his fingers under her collar and escorting her out the door.

Gene dumped the mess kit of food into Skipper's bowl, and when the dog finished his long overdue meal, Gene hooked him to his leash and walked outside into the night.

Every star in the sky twinkled. Gene breathed deeply. It was a mild evening with just a touch of dampness. Skipper's joviality had returned, and he enjoyed the myriad of scents only a dog could discern.

Gene tried to imagine what it must be like for the Allied troops spending their first night on the Normandy beaches. He chose not to dwell on the loss of life that must have occurred. For the time being, it was enough to know that the first day had met with success, whatever the cost.

For several days following the invasion, the Eighth Air Force flew maximum-effort missions deep into enemy territory. Targets were selected to diminish the German army's ability to move troops and supplies from the Russian front to Normandy. The Luftwaffe was pulled out of France and brought back to Germany to defend their homeland.

On June eighth, returning from their twenty-fifth mission, a downcast group sat solemnly on their cots, having little to say to each other. A new directive from General Doolittle had been posted in the latrine. It stated that the thirty-mission tour of combat would be changed effective June sixth. All aircrews that had not completed their thirtieth by D-Day would now continue to fly for the duration of the war.

Gene held his hands to his head. He felt trapped in a

scenario, which could only end in being shot down. *Doolittle must have decided that from this point forward we are all expendable,* he thought.

"Maybe that son of a bitch would like to fly with us," growled Bob.

Conversations with other crews made it clear that there was a pervasive loss of morale.

CHAPTER SEVEN
Skipper Sponsors a Rendezvous

Skipper's romance with Static blossomed, and she seemed to be ever-present in the afternoon when the crew returned from their missions. The two little dogs nuzzled each other, played and sometimes, after an energetic romp, one decided to rest. Invariably, the other would lie down too, with his or her head resting on the other's back.

Gene's mood, so gloomy since Jimmy Doolittle's directive, was lightened by his gratitude that Skipper had someone to play with. Idly, he tossed a rubber bone for both dogs to catch. When they both scrambled after it in a close race, Gene thought to himself, *Maybe I should give Ginny Garwood a call.* He rummaged through the letters on top of his bureau, remembering that she had sent her new address and telephone number from Grove/Wantage Airbase a few days ago. The D-Day excitement had diverted his attention from responding, and he wondered how she was doing in the 27th Air Transport Group as a flight nurse. Before he could talk himself out of it, he ran to the nearest phone.

After dialing the number she had sent in her brief letter, a woman answered. "27th ATG, Sergeant McKewan speaking." He asked for Ginny Garwood.

"I think she's around here somewhere. Just a minute," she replied.

Gene heard laughter, muffled sounds, and soon the awaited familiar voice. "Hi, this is Ginny Garwood. Who am I speaking to?"

"I'm so glad I reached you. This is Gene. Remember me, the pilot who couldn't drive, the guy with the drowned cocker spaniel?"

"How could I forget? How is Skipper? I've told the story a hundred times. It's a great conversation piece."

"He's fine. He has a girlfriend named Static, and they're doing swell. I wish I could say the same for our crew. We just received a directive from Jimmy Doolittle that we'll have to fly for the duration of the war. The thirty-mission cap is a thing of the past!"

"I thought it was twenty-five. When did it become thirty?" Ginny asked.

"Right after you left. That made us feel just great too," he said sarcastically. "But now we're all pretty glum. I was wondering if we could do that dinner we missed before you left. I don't know if I can get a ride to meet you someplace, but I'd like to try. It would be so nice to spend some time with you."

Ginny paused. Gene wasn't sure if she wanted to take the trouble.

"I'm starting a forty-eight hour leave in the morning. I could take a train down and use the time to visit the old infirmary gang. O.K. I'm looking forward to it! See you there at six P.M."

Gene's spirits soared. Thanks to Skipper's mishap, he'd met a girl who was both kind and attractive. It was fortunate that their times off coincided. Flying missions daily since D-Day, he needed a respite.

The next day, alone in the barracks, Gene spread his Class A uniform across his cot. Skipper jumped up to greet him. "Hey, little dog, don't get hair on my 'Sunday best.' I want to make a good impression on the gal who saved your life. Don't you want me to thank her for you?" he asked in his private doggie talk manner. He felt lighthearted for the first time in months. Skipper leaped off the bed as Static approached with a biscuit in her mouth. Skipper watched as she chewed, searching the floor for morsels. "What a good boyfriend you are," said Gene. "Taking whatever crumbs you can get without a scuffle!"

Gat arrived in the middle of Gene's conversation with Skipper. "I guess I'm not da only one who does doggie talk wid him, huh, Lieutenant?"

Gene changed the subject. "Hey, Gat, can you give me a lift to the infirmary in your Jeep? I have to be there by six."

"Shuah, shuah, I can do that!"

Gene jumped into the vehicle, and Gat drove him quickly to the infirmary. The building, bathed in the sunshine of

British summertime, glowed like a beacon promising a pleasant evening.

"Thanks, Gat. I appreciate the lift. See you later. I'll be getting a ride back."

Gat waved with a knowing smile on his face.

As Gene entered the infirmary, he saw Ginny staring out the side window.

Before catching her eye, he noticed her slender figure and softly rounded face. She wore the women's First Class Officer's uniform, a forest green jacket tailored to perfection and a dusty pink skirt ending below the knees, revealing shapely legs. Hearing his steps, she turned toward him, her wide-set eyes expressing warmth. Her shoulder-length light brown hair, curled at the ends, was unexpected, since it had been hidden under her nurse's cap the last time he saw her.

"Thank you for coming. I hope your trip from Wantage went well," he said. He kissed her lightly on the cheek. "You look beautiful."

"The train ride was fine, and I'm glad I came. It's good to see my old friends. I'm starved though. Let's go." She took him by his arm and led him to the Jeep.

The ride to the White Horse Inn, one of the many pubs of its kind, was comfortably quiet. Gene didn't want to make conversation over the noise of the Jeep. It could wait until they were seated.

As they pulled up to the Inn, Ginny asked, "How long has it been, Gene, since that scary day with Skipper?"

"Believe it or not, I remember the exact date. It was May

6th. It's been over a month, and what a month! D-Day was an event that I won't forget as long as l live."

"You'll have to tell me all about it over dinner." She parked the Jeep as close as she could to the Inn and they entered the dark, noisy, smoke-filled interior, the air smelling of beer and fried fish.

A young woman with a flawless, rosy complexion seated them at a table in a corner near a diamond-paned window. "I'll be with you in a moment," she said.

Gene scrutinized the ambiance with interest. The dark-paneled wall on his left, interrupted by a cavernous stone fireplace, lent a medieval quality to the atmosphere. Polished wooden tables, each sporting a candle covered with a glass chimney, provided the only real light in the room. At the far wall, three steps led to a small stage furnished with an upright piano and a microphone. An elaborate bar lined the remaining side.

"This is charming," remarked Ginny. "It's so nice to have a change of scenery, and to experience the local culture." She paused. "I'm also happy to be with Skipper's owner!" she said demurely.

"One of Skipper's owners, but we're more than owners; we're family."

"He must be quite a handful. Where did you get him?" she asked.

Gene compressed the entire saga into a few paragraphs, concluding with their ignoring quarantine orders at Prest-wick. Ginny listened in rapt attention, responding to each event with astonishment. She sighed with relief when hearing how Skipper survived each of the ordeals. "I'm glad to be part of the story," she added.

The plump young woman returned to take their order. "There's not much to choose from, with the rationing and all, but we have a good lamb stew, and, of course, there's always fish and chips."

"I'll have the fish and chips," said Ginny.

"Make that two," said Gene. "I'll also have some beer. How about you, Ginny?"

"I'll try the ale. I've never had it before."

"We'll hurry it along and you'll be served shortly," the young woman answered with a smile.

The hustle and bustle of the pub enveloped Gene in a feeling of buoyancy and good spirits. "How're you doing at the 27th ATG? Have you done any flying yet?"

"We just started flight training. They don't have any airstrips available in Normandy for medical evacuation. In the meantime, they're having to bring the badly wounded back to England on ships. I'm relieved to have the extra time to learn the ropes, but I worry about the GIs who need our help."

He decided to change the subject to something more pleasant. After all, this was a date. "Where's home for you, Ginny?"

"A town you've probably never heard of, Hobart, Indiana, population 18,000. Believe it or not, I'm the oldest of six kids. I got so tired of tending to them that I wanted to be on my own."

"So now you have a whole army of GIs to take care of." Gene laughed.

Ginny smiled. "After I graduated from the nursing program at the University of Indiana, I decided to broaden my professional experience. So here I am. How about you? I know you're from New York. Did you enlist or were you drafted?"

"Oh, I enlisted all right! I had a draft-deferred job in the Norfolk Navy Yard, and I had a helluva time getting a release."

"What were you doing in Norfolk?" she asked.

"It's a long story. Our family needed the income and they paid well. I was trained to be a machinist, which was an important job. My boss refused to let me go."

"So how did you manage to get out?"

"I had to appeal to the Navy captain in command of the machine shop. He thought I was crazy and tried to convince me how important my job was to the war effort. He finally agreed to let me enlist in the Air Corps."

"Are you sorry you didn't stay?"

"I wasn't sorry up until a couple of days ago. But now that we have to fly combat for the duration, I'm having second thoughts."

Ginny was silent. She glanced down with a saddened expression. After a moment, she said, "Well, one good thing. You have an affectionate distraction in Skipper. Maybe that'll help."

The young woman arrived with their food and drinks. Wrapped in newspaper, the crisply fried fish made Gene's mouth water. She placed a large cruet of vinegar in the center of the table.

"I'm starved," said Ginny. "I haven't eaten since breakfast."

They both dug in, savoring the combination of tastes and textures, washing it down with the delicious room-temperature Guinness and Stout.

A chord from the upright piano attracted everyone's attention. Ambling forward to the front of the stage, a short, bony man dressed in a plaid suit, a red bow tie, and a black bowler hat took the microphone. "Welcome to the White Horse Inn. I'm sure you're delighting in a fine meal. Now, will you all join me in singing some of the songs that bring cheer to our hearts during these difficult times?" He shuffled to the piano, and placing his hands on the keys, he played *The White Cliffs of Dover*. His audience sang the words at the top of their lungs, filling the room with love of country and hope for the future. This was followed by *A Nightingale Sang In Barclay Square*.

By the time the second song was completed, the pub was astir with emotion; some laughed, a few cried. Once again the emcee came forward. "I see we have a couple of Yanks here tonight," he said, pointing to Gene and Ginny. "How about a song in their honor? I'm sure you all know *Give My Regards to Broadway*."

The audience belted out the lyrics, as if the words and music were their own. Gene felt a lump in his throat, and he noticed that Ginny wiped a tear from her eye. He took her hand and squeezed it. When the emcee played the last chord, many of the diners stood up and applauded in their direction. After several more songs, the emcee announced an intermission. During the respite, Gene described the DDay effort to Ginny the best way he could.

"It sounds as if the experience was awe-inspiring," she commented.

"For those of us in the air, it was a thrill to be part of such a spectacular moment of history. For the guys on the beaches, it must have been hell."

The waitress appeared with another round of beer and ale. "This one is on the house," she said. Gene thanked her with enthusiasm, and then asked for the check. "We both have busy days tomorrow. I have a mission to fly, and my friend has a long train trip to Grove/Wantage."

Neither of them spoke on the ride back to Great Ashfield, lost in their own thoughts. Ginny pulled up to the barracks, switched off the engine, and reached to take Gene's hand. "Thank you for a lovely evening. I'm so glad I came."

"It meant a lot to me that you wanted to be here."

"Well, all I can say is good luck, God bless, and I hope we'll be able to do it again. Give Skipper a hug for me!"

"I'll do better than that! Wait here just a minute." He hopped out of the Jeep and hurried inside, returning with an excited bundle of fur. "Here's your favorite nurse, Skipper," he said, depositing him on the seat beside Ginny.

She pulled him onto her lap, nuzzling his face. "What a handsome boy you are!" Skipper responded by licking her chin and nose. "I'm counting on you to take care of Gene, and see him through all the missions he has to fly."

Gene leaned over and kissed her goodbye. "Thanks again

for everything. Have a safe trip back," he said, lifting Skipper from her lap.

As Ginny drove off, Gene gazed up into the clear night sky. Every star in the heavens appeared to bear witness to this moment.

CHAPTER EIGHT
Skipper's War Ends

It didn't take long for Gene's heavy-hearted feelings to return. The normalcy experienced with Ginny lasted only a few hours.

After the next day's mission, Gene sat on his bed watching Skipper and Static having a fine time together. "Maybe we should speak to Smitty, Static's owner. What happens to Skipper if we get shot down?" he asked.

"You're right! We don't know how many more missions we'll have to fly before this damn war is over," said Bob.

"It shouldn't be Smitty! We have to sit down with Gat and talk it through with him," countered J.O. "He would be hurt if he found out that we had approached someone else. He's as close to Skipper as we are!"

"Gat won't want to talk about it. He thinks we're immortal!" said Gene. "Let's put it on the backburner for a day or two."

Much to everyone's surprise, Doolittle's disheartening orders were suddenly replaced with a new directive:

All crews who did not finish their tour of combat on June sixth will return to the United States upon completion of their thirtieth mission. They will have one month Rest and Recuperation, after which they will rejoin their Bomb Groups and fly for the duration.

"It's a bone," said Al. "They're buying us off."

"It looks like General Jimmy is having to calm the troubled waters," said Bob.

"Whatever. It's better than a kick in the ass," said Gene. He was still angry and saw little humor in their remarks. Nevertheless, the prospect of going home for an extended visit helped to soften the long-term outlook.

On the morning of June twenty-first, Gene awoke feeling excited. Today they would complete their tour of combat. He lifted Skipper into the air and said, "You're going home for Rest and Recuperation and some good old American cooking, little pal. You only have to give us luck one more time." This was followed with a noisy kiss on both ears.

On the way to the briefing, Gene enjoyed the lighthearted banter in the truck. Bob joked, "Al, you can take a nap on this milk-run. It'll be a shorty for our thirtieth."

"Yeah," Al replied, "it'll be nice to stretch without crouching behind the armor plating to duck the flak."

When the lights were dimmed in the Ready Room, the slide projector showed:

"TARGET FOR TODAY"

It was followed in large black letters by one word:

"BERLIN"

Gene swallowed hard. His crewmates gasped. It seemed unconscionable for Operations to have scheduled them to attack the most heavily defended target in Europe.

Twelve hundred Fortresses and Liberators participated in the ten-hour mission. Hundreds of radar-controlled antiaircraft guns threw up barrages that turned daytime into night. Their plane literally rocked from the concussion of exploding shells, and flak damage was extensive.

When Gene heard Al's voice on the intercom shouting "Bombs Away," he began singing a song he remembered from childhood.

> "Pack up all my care and woe,
> Here I go, singing low,
> Bye, bye, Blackbird!"

Scores of American long-range fighters escorted the bombers on the return flight.

Thirty missions!

They were finally given the traditional honor of buzzing

the runway and tower while firing flares. The rest of the formation landed, allowing J.O.'s crew to be in the spotlight, a day they'd thought might never come.

Captain Warren Cerrone, the Squadron Operations Officer, was waiting to greet them at their hardstand. "Congratulations," he said. "This is a great event for you men and for the 550th Bomb Squadron."

"We made it!" Al said. "Peggy's prayers worked. Her rosary beads must be worn out."

The crew hugged each other like a baseball team that had just won the World Series. No one discussed what might lay ahead after the respite back in the States.

Shortly, they received orders directing them to Liverpool for ocean transport to the United States. After thirty days Rest and Recuperation, they would report to the Ritz Carlton Hotel in Atlantic City, New Jersey before returning to England.

While they were relaxing in the Officers Club, J.O. raised a subject no one had considered. "How are we going to deal with Skipper on a troopship?"

"Same way we've been doing it all along," said Al.

"We don't have a clue what the mess hall setup will be like on an ocean liner, to say nothing of where the hell we'll walk him—or *if* we can walk him," said Gene.

"One thing's for sure," said Bob. "We better find enough food to last at least a week in case we run into a problem."

J.O. interrupted. "This is getting too complicated. We've managed so far. As long as we eat, he'll eat too."

Gene felt uncomfortable with the uncertainty of what

might lie ahead, but he decided to let the subject pass. After they left the Officers Club, he packed up his bags and looked around the barracks, his home for the past four months. Handshakes and exchanges of good luck to the remaining bunkmates, tinged with the ever-present reality that some might not be there when he returned, put a cloak of sadness over the otherwise joyous occasion.

Gat arrived on the scene. "Youse guys ain't gettin' outa heah widout me saying goodbye."

He stood there awkwardly for a brief moment and then, with a swift motion, scooped up Skipper from J.O.'s cot and cuddled him to his broad chest, like a little boy holding a beloved teddy bear. For several moments, he mumbled his farewell words into Skipper's ear. "I'm gonna miss ya, you little pest. We had a lot of fun togedda, didn't we? Just rememba everything I taught ya."

Gene was touched to see a tear roll down the side of Gat's face. He had spent more time with Skipper than they had. Gat turned away from them and with a backward wave said, "See youse guys in a couple of months," as he hurried out the door.

CHAPTER NINE
Skipper's Voyage

The hustle and bustle at London's Euston Station was the typical mix of people in a wartime setting, with soldiers saying goodbye, families waving, and commuters going to work.

Gene held Skipper on a short leash and guided him onto the train and into one of the compartments. The space was already occupied by a middle-aged couple, who cordially greeted the foursome as they squeezed in beside them.

The woman's face lit up when she saw Skipper, who was trembling in the strange environment.

"Oh, what a handsome litt'l fella you are," she said, lifting Skipper onto her ample lap.

Her husband, a heavyset, well-groomed gentleman, asked, "Where would the four of you be going?"

"Liverpool," answered J.O. "And from there, we board a ship to the United States."

"We just completed a tour of bombing missions with the Eighth Air Force," added Al.

"Congratulations! You were lucky, you were, from what we've heard!" said the man.

"And you're taking this litt'l love with you?" asked the woman, kissing the spot between Skipper's ears.

"We've had him since he was eight weeks old, and there's no way that we'll leave him behind," said J.O.

Gene was once again reminded of the difficulties that might arise.

As if the man could read his mind, he said, "We have a litt'l Border Terrier, and I can't imagine how we'd deal with him on an ocean voyage, what with the feedin' and walkin' and all."

Gene nodded in agreement. A seed of worry began to grow rapidly in the back of his head.

"Where did you get this litt'l dog?" asked the man.

"It's a long story," said J.O. "Too long to describe."

By the time they reached Lime Street Station in Liverpool, Gene felt as comfortable with this couple as if they had been old friends.

"We would enjoy hearing from you. I'll be worrying about the litt'l pup's voyage across the ocean," said the woman. "Derek, write our address on that newspaper."

Derek scribbled rapidly and handed the scrap to J.O. "God bless and good luck. Thanks for being with us."

They divided themselves into two of the taxicabs queued

up at the railroad station. Gene held Skipper, who poked his head outside the window, ears flapping, nose raised in exploration of the mélange of aromas flooding his nostrils as they neared the waterfront.

Salty sea breezes aroused Gene's sense of adventure, and despite the lengthy train ride, he felt energized at the prospect of a steamship voyage across the Atlantic.

They were directed to the convoy area by an obliging dockside worker. There, they located the S.S. *United States*, a converted luxury ocean liner, resting in its berth.

Crowds of officers, enlisted men, and WACs milled about a one-story pre-fab building. Bob pointed to a large sign above the entrance that read: "United States Military Personnel Check In Here."

"Why don't you go and sign in for us, J.O.? You have all of our orders. We'll stay out here with Skipper."

It was almost an hour before J.O. returned, his face somber, his mouth tightened in an expression of concern. "What's up?" asked Gene. "You look like someone canceled our leave."

"It's worse than that. They're not allowing pets aboard the ship."

"Ugh. This is where we came in," said Al.

"It never ends!" moaned Bob.

"The first thing we have to do is figure out how we're going to sneak him aboard. Once we get him into the cabin, we'll be home free," said Gene.

"That's if he doesn't bark at people walking through the corridor," said Bob.

"Let's take one worry at a time. I have room in my duffel bag. We'll put him in there and I'll sling it over my shoulder." Gene unbuckled his bag and gently placed Skipper on top of his folded underwear. "You'll be O.K., little dog. I know it's hot in there, but it won't be for long, hopefully."

With J.O. leading the way, Gene carefully positioned himself between Bob and Al in order to camouflage his little stowaway as they walked up the gangplank.

On deck, J.O. presented their papers to a smiling petty officer, who welcomed them aboard. While he was checking their cabin assignment, a muffled whine came from the duffel bag. In alarm, Gene covered the sound by coughing and wheezing.

"You better get yourself some water, Lieutenant," said the sailor, pointing to the corridor. "Your cabin's just down the hall past the dining room."

They opened the door to a cramped space arranged to accommodate sixteen men in four stacks of bunks, which resembled storage shelves in a warehouse.

"This ain't too bad," said Bob. "We even have a porthole."

"I wonder how many more guys are gonna be in here with us," said Gene, predicting more problems with Skipper.

"There may not be any more," said J.O., "because I heard one of the staff in the check-in office saying that there would only be about four hundred passengers, and the ship is rigged to handle over two thousand."

"We deserve a little bit of luck," said Bob.

Released from the duffel bag, Skipper ran from bunk to bunk in a frantic exploration of his strange new quarters.

An announcement came over the P.A. system. "All passengers are required to attend an indoctrination discussion in the ship's main lounge at 0400."

"I'll meet you guys down there after I scrounge some toilet paper from the latrine in case Skipper messes in the cabin while we're gone," said Gene.

This oughta do it for the whole trip, he thought, collecting two rolls and tucking them into his duffel bag. He lifted Skipper onto one of the lower berths along with a few of his toys.

"We'll be back soon, Skipper, and you better be a good boy. And don't bark!"

The ship's main lounge was a spacious open area. Although the walls were lavishly decorated with handpainted murals of seascapes and European scenes, the furnishings were typically Army. The elaborate indirect lighting cast shadows on the crude folding chairs lined up in rows on the stylized carpeting.

Crowds of enlisted men, women, and officers jammed the area facing the platform on which were seated several Army and Navy brass. A lanky, weathered Navy captain stepped up to the microphone and cleared his throat to command attention.

"I'd like to welcome all of you aboard the S.S. *United States.* We're sailing in a convoy with many other ships, and we'll be escorted by destroyers and destroyer escorts of the U.S. Navy. Normally, the voyage for a ship like this would take approximately six days, but because of the danger of German submarine attacks, our varied and evasive course will require more time. We must also reduce our speed to equal the slowest freighter in the group.

"Our capacity as a troopship can accommodate upwards of two thousand. Although we have few luxuries aboard, you'll find the quarters to be relatively comfortable since we are sailing with only four hundred passengers.

"There are day rooms and dining rooms for officers and enlisted personnel. Everyone should read the bulletin boards, which are located in various places throughout ship and describe meal hours and times for using community fresh water showers. We also have a theater with a selection of films that we hope you'll enjoy. Now, I'd like to turn the microphone over to Colonel McDonald, who will be our ship's military commanding officer during this voyage." He stepped aside as he gestured to the man next to him. "Colonel McDonald."

The colonel, his uniform replete with eagles on his shoulders and a chest full of service ribbons, stood silently for a few moments, making eye contact with his audience. Gene could feel the authority of his presence. His steel gray eyes, jutting jaw, and stiff posture projected the impression of a tough, demanding career officer. Gene could imagine him painstakingly trimming his thin white mustache to add to his immaculate appearance.

"First, let me join Captain Curtis in welcoming you aboard this beautiful ship.

"It's important for all of you to understand that this is not a pleasure cruise. We have to regard the entire Atlantic Ocean as enemy waters and know that we'll be constantly exposed to submarine attack throughout the crossing. It is mandatory that you observe the following disciplines:

"Number one: Blackout during the evening hours must be scrupulously adhered to. There will be no smoking on outside decks and walkways. One match or one exposed light can put this entire convoy at risk. Portholes must be covered after dark. In fact, to avoid oversights, it would be best to keep them covered around the clock.

"Number two: There will be frequent submarine and fire drills, which everyone must attend."

Gene and Al exchanged worried glances, each of them aware of what the other was thinking.

The colonel continued. "Number three: All outside decks will be constantly policed from dusk to dawn, and any infraction of the blackout rules will result in serious discipline.

"There'll be junior officers assigned to supervise all enlisted personnel areas, and any altercations or serious problems will be brought to my attention. Are there any questions?" He waited a brief moment. "Since there are none, you are all dismissed."

Immediately following the briefing, a crescendo of voices rose up and Gene picked up bits of conversation as he moved through the crowd on his way to the stateroom.

"Oh, God. I can't button my skirt anymore. I'll be glad to get into maternity clothes," said a short, square-looking brunette.

"How do you think your folks are gonna take the news?" asked a tall blond private in the Women's Army Corps. "I dread telling mine that I'm pregnant. Joey and I aren't even married yet." They were talking with three other WACs who seemed to be in the same predicament.

"It was hell on that beach. It was hell on that beach," repeated a corporal over and over, his eyes staring and his face expressionless.

Another private nodded. "D-Day, Death Day."

Gene hurried past them, feeling thankful that he fought in the air and not on the ground.

"What the hell happens to Skipper if, God forbid, we get hit by a torpedo and have to abandon ship?" Al was saying when Gene stepped into the room.

"The problem is, how can we hang on to him?" asked Bob.

"It wouldn't be a *we*. One of us would have to deal with him."

"Oh, I'll take care of that," said J.O. "But if I had to jump overboard, there's no way I could hold on to him."

"We'll have to work out some sort of rig to tie him to you," said Gene. "I wonder where we could get a few feet of rope."

"I know." Bob jumped up from his bunk. "I'll be back in a few minutes," he said, slamming the door behind him.

"Come 'ere, Skipper. I wanna see something." J.O. lifted Skipper onto his bunk. "Maybe we can use a couple of our web belts for a makeshift harness. You hold onto him, Gene."

Skipper cocked his head. "What's going on here?" he seemed to ask.

"It's okay, little buddy; this could save your life," said J.O., tying a belt under Skipper's front paws. "Great! There's plenty of room left over to knot it, but we need another belt."

Bob returned to the room holding a coil of rope. "Look what I dug up!" he said, smiling broadly. He dropped it on the bunk next to Skipper and pulled a web belt out of his musette bag. When they finished the harness, there was just enough rope left to tie around J.O.'s waist.

"Don't worry, little dog, I'll take care of you," J.O. said, scratching Skipper's ears.

"Let's hope we never have to use it," said Gene, unhooking the harness.

A loud blast from the ship's horn signaled their departure from the pier. "I want to go out and watch," said Bob. They left Skipper on a bunk, shut the door securely behind them, and hurried to the foredeck railing.

Tugboats on the port and starboard sides nudged the ship into the middle of the Mersey River, where the vessel's powerful engines took over.

"Wow! That's something, how those little tugs can push a big ship like this, isn't it?" Gene said.

"Yeah. Kinda reminds me of how Skipper bosses us around!" J.O. chuckled.

"You got that right," Bob said.

A warm, stiff breeze churned the water into choppy waves as they left the Mersey and entered the Irish Sea, where a group of Navy destroyers and other ships were organizing into a convoy.

"Now there's a reassuring sight," said Gene. *How lucky we are to be on our way home,* he thought.

"Hey, it's six o'clock. It's time for dinner. Let's see what the dining room is like," said Al.

"I've gotta get the mess kit for Skipper's supper. Meet you down there," said Gene.

When Skipper saw Gene, he grabbed his rubber bone, forepaws stretched, rump raised, tail wagging. It was as if everything was A.O.K., and he wanted to play.

"Not now, little dog. I'll be back with some chow real soon, and then we'll play." Skipper stopped. His eyes were full of love, and his lips curled back in a smile. Gene rushed out without a backward glance.

The stairway entrance to the dining room was dramatic, with its wide steps and deep blue sculptured carpeting. Gene could imagine cruise passengers in tuxedos and ball gowns making their grand entrances. He was thoroughly surprised to see round tables covered with crisp white linen cloths and set for eight with sparkling cutlery. No chow lines here.

A slightly built, stern-faced Navy lieutenant was standing to one side at the landing, having a heated discussion with one of the dining room orderlies.

"Good evening, Lieutenant," said Gene. "This place is fabulous. It's like entering the Empire Room at the Waldorf Astoria."

"This is a military dining room, not a hotel," the Navy officer snapped.

What a grouch, Gene thought. *Maybe he doesn't like Army people.* He spied Al, Bob, and J.O. seated at a table with four other Air Corps officers.

"Meet Jim, Mike, Dave, and Guy from the 91st Bomb Group," said Bob. "This is Gene, our co-pilot." He shook hands with each of them and sat down, placing his napkin over the mess kit on his lap.

Dining room orderlies emerged from the kitchen wheeling carts of food. Gene was delighted to see platters of succulent sliced leg of lamb and gravy, fluffy mashed potatoes, and green beans with carrots. Two baskets of dinner rolls accompanied the family style service.

"Wow, the garlic in that meat is delicious," Gene said. "They're really treating us like royalty."

"This ain't hard to take," said Al.

"Can you believe? No Spam," added Bob.

They all dug in, relishing their unexpected feast. Gene wondered if this festive dining would continue or if it was just a "welcome aboard" offering. He made sure he got his share of seconds before the platters were emptied.

Without thinking, he removed the mess kit from his lap and placed it on the table. Bob caught Gene's eyes with an accusing stare.

Uh-oh, thought Gene. *This is dumb.* He dumped his plate of seconds into the mess kit anyway. No one commented.

Soon, the orderlies returned with carts laden with a variety of cookies and slices of multi-flavored brick ice cream.

Guy looked at Gene. "Too bad you can't take some of this ice cream back with you."

"But I'll help myself to some of these cookies," said Gene, slipping a handful into the side pocket of his jacket.

After dinner, tired from the long day, all of them opted to pass on the evening's movie and hurried back to the stateroom.

As soon as they entered with the garlic-scented mess kit, Skipper stood on his hind legs in a vigorous performance of his song and dance routine. "Shh, shh, shh, shh. No song. No, no, no!" Gene placed the mess kit on the floor, and Skipper devoured its contents, relishing the gravy-soaked lamb and licking his chops.

"What are we going to do about getting Skipper some fresh air and exercise?" asked Al. "To say nothing of minimizing his messing on the floor."

"What d'ya say we explore the deck areas near our cabin?" suggested Gene.

"I'll go with you," said J.O.

They were surprised no one was on watch near the doorway and walked toward the stern of the ship. No one there either, but J.O. pointed to sailors on the open deck above, stationed strategically on either side of the vessel.

"It looks as though we can sneak him out here maybe between eleven and midnight. If we're careful to stay between the doorway and the stern, we can probably avoid being noticed by the sailors up there."

"We'll have to walk fast, or else he won't get enough exercise."

They decided that Gene would go first. The other three would take their turns on succeeding nights.

Everyone stretched out on their bunks, and Gene, with hands clasped behind his head, was aware of the gentle rolling motion of the ship. He mentally rehearsed his foray out on deck with Skipper, cautioning himself to be hyper-alert and to stay within easy access of the doorway.

At ten-thirty, anxious to have the episode behind him, Gene folded many sheets of toilet paper into a flat wad and stuffed it into the side pocket of his jacket. "Well, here goes nothing," he announced, hooking Skipper to his leash.

"Good luck," said J.O.

"Have fun," Al grinned.

Gene peeked out the door. When he was satisfied that he had a clear path, he hurried to the exit. "We're going for a nice walk," he whispered, lowering Skipper onto the moist deck.

The sky was moonless, and the blackout conditions created an eerie darkness. It was difficult to see ahead. Hidden from the deck above, Gene moved briskly along the railing, gently pulling on the leash with Skipper trotting to keep up. Suddenly, Skipper stopped and began turning in circles before arching his back and squatting. Just then, Gene heard footsteps.

"I'll check the stern," a voice said.

Gene tucked Skipper under his arm and raced down the passageway back to the room, opened the door, and tossed him in.

"I'll be back in a minute!" he said, unraveling the wad of toilet paper in his pocket. In the dark, he couldn't see where Skipper had left his deposit. He dropped to his knees and ran his hand over the deck.

"Did you lose something, sir?" a sailor asked.

"I think I dropped a small brown leather key case when I was out here earlier."

"You'll have a tough time finding it without some light. We'll be out here until daylight, and if we find it, we'll bring it to your cabin. What's the number?"

"Two sixty-five," Gene answered reluctantly.

"Got it," the sailor said, sauntering away.

Oh no, Gene thought. *I've got to find his turds before one of those guys steps in it and figures out we've got a dog in two sixty-five.* After a few minutes, he started sniffing the air, when the hand with the toilet paper in it touched a warm, damp lump. He scooped it up and tossed it overboard.

Heading immediately back to the cabin, he encountered J.O. as soon as he opened the door.

"Hey, look at your pants. They're filthy!" J.O. said. "What was all the commotion about? What the hell were you doin' out there?"

"I don't want to talk about it now," he said, stripping off his uniform. "We'll discuss it in the morning." He kicked the heap of clothes under his bunk and flopped down on top of the mattress.

"I wish I could've been a fly on the wall out there," J.O. said, lifting Skipper up beside him. "You sure are a full-time job, little fella." He switched off the light.

Gene was dozing off when J.O. shouted, "Phew! He's blowing garlic breath right in my face!"

Gene laughed in spite of himself. "That's nothing compared to what I went through!"

* * *

During the next few days, the weather was clear with moonlit nights. Meals continued to be superb, and Gene settled into an easy routine. When he thought back to the daily dose of aerial combat in the skies over Europe, this voyage was soothing regardless of the undercurrent of danger.

However, on the morning of the fourth day, the weather turned ugly. Green-gray waves were running eight to ten feet high, topped with whitecaps. The ship's roll was more pronounced, making it necessary to walk at an angle in the corridors and on deck. Gene was fascinated at the sight of the destroyers and small destroyer escorts plunging nose down and almost disappearing in the troughs of the waves. He wondered how their crews could tolerate the violent motion without getting seasick.

At lunch, in the middle of sprinkling parmesan cheese over his savory spaghetti and meat sauce, Gene was startled by a loud blast of horns signaling a submarine alert. Everyone raced to their quarters and grabbed their life preservers. Skipper was cowering alongside the regurgitated remains of last night's supper.

"Ugh! We'll have to clean this up later and pray he doesn't walk in it," Al said.

"Quick, let's get his harness on," J.O. said.

Gene snatched it from under his mattress and strapped it around the dog.

"See you soon, Skipper. Don't worry," said J.O., placing him on the foot of his bunk.

The skies were still cloud-covered, but the height of the waves had diminished, and now Gene was able to see vigorous activity on the decks of the escorts. Depth charges, resembling ash cans, were dropped off the sides and stems of the destroyers. Gene was jarred by the explosions beneath the surface, which reverberated against the hull of their ship. It was as if they had suffered several direct hits.

"This is no drill," said a somber J.O.

Gene studied the surface of the water, nervously watching for the telltale signs of approaching torpedoes. His heart raced while the booming of the depth charges continued. The feeling was the same as when German antiaircraft shells exploded around his airplane.

"This would be some finale—thirty missions and then sunk by a German submarine on the way home," said Bob.

There were several minutes of silence, then finally the "All Clear" was sounded.

"Back to our cold spaghetti," laughed Dave of the 91st, who happened to be standing nearby.

"I'll pass," said Gene. "I'm gonna grab some sack time in the cabin. See you at dinner."

The others made similar excuses, and all four returned to their stateroom.

They found Skipper trembling beneath J.O.'s bunk. "Poor little boy. You're having one helluva dog day, aren't you?" said Bob, picking him up and cuddling him in his arms.

Along with the dated movies, mealtimes became the highlight of each day. With Skipper adjusting to his surroundings and nocturnal promenades, the nervousness about caring for him aboard ship dissipated.

On the evening of the seventh day, Gene looked at his watch in anticipation of another gourmet eating experience. "Ding-a-ling," he announced. "Ding-a-ling, everyone. Dinner is now being served in the main dining room!"

"You guys go ahead. I'm at a real good part of this chapter, and I want to finish it," said Bob, indicating the book in his hand.

The others left Bob in his bunk and made their way to the dining room, which was filling up. "Good evening, Lieutenant," said Gene to the mess officer. "Wild time out there, wasn't it?"

"Par for the course," was the chilly response.

J.O., Gene, and Al exchanged glances.

"I wonder what it would take to get that guy to smile," said J.O.

"Maybe he suffers from chronic heartburn," Al said.

The orderlies had already begun serving. Gene still couldn't believe the delectable quality of their dinners. Tonight there were platters of turkey, cranberry sauce, and sweet potatoes.

"How 'bout this?" said Al. "We're having a Thanksgiving dinner in July."

"Where's Bob?" asked Mike of the 91st.

"He'll be along in a couple of minutes," said J.O.

"Here he comes now," said Al, pointing to the stairway across the dining room.

Gene turned. What he thought he saw was terrifying. *It can't be. Dear God, it can't be!* For there, toddling down the steps behind Bob, was a black and gold ball of fur. Skipper.

Gene frantically pointed to Bob in a downward direction. J.O. shut his eyes and shook his head in horror.

Bob looked to see if his pants were unzipped with his palms raised questioningly.

Gene said in a loud whisper, "Skipper's behind you!"

Bob wheeled around to see the angry mess officer grab Skipper under his front legs. Pulsating jets of pee streamed from the terrified little dog as the outraged lieutenant sprinted across the room and up the stairs, holding him with arms thrust forward.

Nervous laughter ran throughout the dining room as the officer disappeared. Gene sat motionless, his insides churning. There was no doubt that Skipper would be tossed overboard.

Gene had visions of Skipper's head bobbing in the gray waves of the North Atlantic, desperately paddling to survive, eyes searching for his big friends. *How,* thought Gene, *can such a tragic end befall the little dog that has been our good luck charm through thirty combat missions? He doesn't deserve this. Why does he have to pay with his life for decisions made by four grown men?* He would gladly forgo his trip home and climb back into the cockpit of his B-17 tomorrow if it would save Skipper.

Gene looked again at Bob. The expression of sadness on Bob's face made him feel some compassion but didn't ease the pain. The talk in the dining room dropped to a murmur, as if everyone recognized the seriousness of the event.

A scratchy sound of static from the Public Address System interrupted Gene's morbid thoughts. "Now hear this! Now hear this!" slowly announced a stern, militant voice on the P.A. "If the Air Corps Officers who own the black cocker spaniel would like to save their dog's life, they should report to the ship's commanding officer immediately. I repeat, if the

Air Corps Officers who own the black cocker spaniel would like to save their dog's life, they should report to the ship's commanding officer immediately."

"Thank God," said Bob, tilting his face upward with a sigh of relief. "I'll go to the colonel's office. It's all my fault that this happened. I just wasn't careful to shut the door when I left the stateroom. I didn't have a clue that he was following me."

"No, Bob. I'll handle this. Skipper is my responsibility, and I'll have to answer for all of the violations since we left Presque Isle," said J.O.

"All four of us have been involved from the very beginning, and we should all take the heat together," said Gene. "We'll let J.O. do the talking, and we'll be there for support." They marched out of the dining room, while heads turned to watch the foursome go to meet their fate.

Entering the colonel's office, they spotted a trembling Skipper tied to the leg of a leather upholstered chair in a corner of the room. Lining themselves abreast, they snapped to attention and smartly saluted the colonel.

"Sir, we are the owners of that little dog," said J.O., pointing to Skipper, "and we're reporting to you in accordance with the announcement."

There was an oppressive silence as the colonel's eyes darted from one officer to the other. Gene studied the colonel's face. His mustache seemed to bristle. "Is it reasonable for me to assume that you brought this dog aboard the ship despite the well-posted regulations banning pets?"

"Yes, sir," answered J.O.

The colonel's face reddened with anger. "I'm sure the four

of you understand that disciplinary action could include court martial."

"Yes, sir," they all answered.

The colonel's fingers drummed nervously on the top of his desk. He looked up. "You mean to say that you all risked court martial to take a dog back to the United States with you?"

"We're not just taking him back with us, sir," said J.O. "We're bringing him home again to where he came from."

"*What?*" shouted the colonel, his eyes squinting in disbelief. "You've been violating regulations since you left the States?"

"Yes, sir," answered J.O. "We tried to send Skipper home when we were in Gander Lake, Newfoundland. But the lady in charge of the Red Cross Office said they would take Skipper out and shoot him after we left. We've had him since he was eight weeks old, sir, and all through combat training in Florida. That's how we ended up in the predicament we're in now."

The colonel leaned back, shaking his head. He sat tight-lipped with a look of frustration and exasperation.

He removed a pen and a lined yellow legal pad from the drawer of his desk. "What Bomb Group are you presently assigned to?"

"The 385th Bomb Group, 550th Squadron at Great Ashfield, sir," answered J.O.

The colonel scribbled the details with his scratchy fountain pen. "How many missions did you fly?"

"Thirty, sir."

"When did you complete your tour of combat?"

"On June 21st, sir."

"Did you take part in the D-Day operation?"

"Yes, sir. We bombed Omaha Beach twenty minutes before our troops came ashore, and later that evening we flew a support mission for the British and Canadian troops outside of Caen."

"Any of you ever wounded?"

"Yes, sir," answered J.O. "Our tailgunner lost part of his left leg on our second mission, and I was wounded in the shoulder in a raid over Augsburg. We came back with over two hundred and fifty holes in our plane, and it had to be scrapped."

"Where did they send you on your thirtieth mission?"

"To Berlin, sir," answered J.O.

The colonel put his pen down. He shifted his eyes to the still-cowering Skipper. With an audible sigh, he said, "Take your little dog and get the hell out of my office before I change my mind."

"I'll never forget this, sir."

"Thank you, sir."

"You just don't know what this dog means to us," Gene said to the colonel.

"Oh, yes I do," he responded.

"How about a nice song and dance for the colonel?" said Gene, untying Skipper from the chair.

Skipper began pirouetting on his hind legs and yelping joyously. His head was held high as if he understood the importance of the moment.

Colonel McDonald couldn't resist a chuckle as he reached

down and patted Skipper's head. Gene tucked him under his arm, and they scooted out of the office.

Bounding down the corridor, they heard the colonel yell after them, "One more thing. Keep that dog out of the Officers' dining room!"

"Yes, sir," they shouted.

Skipper became an instant celebrity aboard the ship. At breakfast the following morning, everyone crowded around their table with congratulatory handshakes, laughter, and back slaps. The story of Skipper's odyssey was told over and over.

The first time the group walked him on the open decks, they were besieged by sailors, who engulfed the little star with displays of joyful affection.

"I sure wish I could bring you home to my little son! He would love you," said one of the sailors.

"You've had a war all your own, little feller," said a lanky seaman, roughing up Skipper's head.

In response, Skipper paraded as if he were competing at a dog show, lifting his paws and glancing from left to right, obviously enjoying all of the attention.

Among the admirers, Gene recognized the two sailors on watch the first night he walked Skipper. "Did you ever find that brown key case, Lieutenant?" asked one of them, catching Gene's eye while smiling mischievously.

Gene laughed. "I sure did. I saved you the trouble."

From the moment of Skipper's appearance, food flowed from every source. Bones, cut up steak, shredded chicken, and slices of bacon were brought to their table by dining room orderlies. Even the mess officer smiled sheepishly as he observed his subordinates bringing their offerings to the four caretakers.

The final days were the most relaxed of the voyage. On the morning of the tenth day, having been advised that they would be entering New York Harbor early in the morning, Gene was up and dressed at sunrise.

"C'mon, Skipper, let's walk. This'll be a big day for all of us."

Topside shadows of the railings were reflected on the deck, creating a patterned path for their walk. Flocks of seagulls circled above, signaling the approaching landfall. Skipper pulled on his leash, barking at a gull perched atop one of the stanchions. He was nearly a year old and had grown from puppyhood into a sleek, well-formed young adult with golden markings in contrast to his shiny black coat. Gene was heavy-hearted knowing that soon J.O. would be taking him back to South Carolina. None of them had discussed the separation. Walking around the deck, Gene reflected on the events that had absorbed their lives.

"If only you could talk, Skipper. What stories you could tell! We sure got through it together though, all of us."

They returned to their room to find the others packing their bags.

"Did you have a nice walk, little buddy?" Bob asked with what sounded like a catch in his throat.

"I'm gonna miss you, little guy," Al said, taking Skipper in his arms and burying his face in his fur. He nuzzled Skipper's curly ears and kissed his forehead a dozen times before putting him down. "I'll bring you back some goodies for breakfast," he choked.

"Breakfast," Bob repeated, pulling a handkerchief out of his pocket as he headed for the corridor.

After their final dining experience, they took up positions at the forward railings to get a good view. Gene drank in the much-heralded skyline of his native New York, basking in the warmth of the early July sun. He thought of John Demereaux and so many other fellow airmen who went down in flames. There would be no homecoming like this for those men, and he felt guilty even while appreciating his own good fortune.

Sturdy tugs maneuvered the ship into its berth. They gathered their gear, collected travel vouchers, and proceeded down the gangplank with Skipper pulling on the leash in J.O.'s hand.

Gene knelt on the dock. "Goodbye, little pal. I love you, Skipper, and I'll never forget you." He let Skipper put his paws on his shoulders so his pink tongue could lap his face. "Be a good boy, and take care of J.O." With that, he ruffled Skipper's ears and stood up, extending his hand to J.O.

"See you guys in Atlantic City in four weeks." He turned and walked toward a line of taxis, tears flowing down both cheeks.

"Where to, Lieutenant?" asked the cab driver as Gene tossed his two bags into the back seat.

"526 West 111th Street, right off Broadway."

The driver turned the cab onto the West Side Highway,

only to exit a few minutes later onto 34th Street, one of Manhattan's major crosstown arteries.

It was almost noon on a typically hot July day, and traffic moved slowly. Gene gazed at the young women window-shopping in their sleeveless dresses. Men with their suit jackets flapping, neckties loosened, and collars unbuttoned hurried along the sidewalk. *Little do they know how fortunate they are to have been spared the devastating raids suffered by the English people,* he thought.

Turning left onto Herald Square, the cab slowed to a crawl opposite Macy's main entrance. Was it only four months ago he and Al took Skipper to buy him a sweater in the pet department? Or was it a lifetime ago?

The line of traffic picked up speed. He'd be home in a few minutes, but his visit would only be an intermission in a war still to be fought, with victory now on the horizon.

Gene, Janice, and their Dad
30 Days R & R

EPILOGUE

J.O.'s family was delighted to take custody of Skipper for the duration of the war. It was reported that he refused meals of dog food and continued to entertain everyone with his "song and dance" routine.

Only the officers returned to England after the month's Rest and Recuperation.

Al, J.O., and Bob flew five more missions and returned once again to assignments at Stateside Air Bases.

Gene accepted a post as a C-47 transport pilot with the Headquarters Wing of the United States Strategic Air Forces. He stayed in Europe throughout the last year of the war, flying resupply missions to the front lines and retrieving wounded soldiers, liberated prisoners of war, concentration camp survivors, and slave laborers of varied nationalities.

Dogs were to be important members of Gene's family for decades following the war, but there would always be a special corner of his heart reserved for a small, soft black and gold cocker spaniel, whose unconditional love and foolishness did so much to calm the fears and lift the spirits of four young Army Air Corps fliers during what was certainly the most traumatic experience of their lives.

About the Authors

Eugene Hackel lost his mother when he was sixteen and became the main breadwinner for his family during the Depression because his father, as a musician, was unable to find work. Eugene was exempted from the draft due to his employment at the Virginia shipyards, but he insisted on joining the Air Force to fight for his country and was reluctantly granted permission. After World War II he went into the textile business.

Serene Hackel has been an elementary school teacher, an addiction counselor, and a writer, as well as a wife and a mother. She has a degree in Theater and master's degrees in both Education and Counseling Psychology.

After writing *Skipper Goes to War* with her husband Eugene, Serene went on to write her own novels. The first to be published, in 2017, was *Becoming Us, 1900-1925: A Family Grows with America*. It is drawn from the true stories her mother told Serene about the experiences of her grandparents, her mother, and her siblings throughout a turbulent quarter-century of change.

Serene is currently a resident of West Hartford, Connecticut, where she continues to write and to make appearances speaking about her books. She can be contacted through eFitzgeraldPublishing@gmail.com.

Made in the USA
San Bernardino, CA
18 July 2019